Praise for

Encounters with God

"A friend recently asked me, "Do miracles still happen today?" I'm grateful to now have this book as an answer. By featuring a variety of people, circumstances, and troubles, Alexandra's book powerfully testifies to how, "There are different kinds of working, but in all of them and in everyone it is the same God at work" (1 Corinthians 12:6). My hope is that every reader is drawn closer to God through faith in Jesus by the same powerful Spirit!"

----Pastor Paul Horstmeyer
   Site Pastor
   Trinity Kimberly Way

Encounters with God

A collection of true stories of healings, knowings, answers to prayer, and other uncanny events

ALEXANDRA GEORGAS

Encounters with God

By Alexandra Georgas

© Copyright 2024 Alexandra Georgas
ISBN 979-8-218-50055-9

All rights reserved. No part of this publication may be reproduced, stored in a retrieval system, or transmitted in any form or by any means – electronic, mechanical, photocopied, recording, or any other – except for brief quotations in printed reviews, without the prior written permission of the author.

Scriptures noted NIV are taken from the New International Version. Copyright 1973, 1978, 1984, 1989. The Zondervan Corporation.

Scriptures noted ESV are taken from the English Standard Version. Copyright 2010. Crossway.

Scriptures noted NLT are taken from the New Living Translation. Copyright 2007. Tyndale House Publishers.

Scriptures noted KJV are taken from the King James Version. Copyright 1976, 1978. Moody Bible Institute of Chicago.

Scriptures noted NASB are taken from the New American Standard Bible. Copyright 1981. Holman Bible Publishers.

Scriptures noted TLB are taken from The Living Bible. Copyright 1971. Tyndale House Publishers.

Published by
Alexandra Georgas
www.alexandrageorgas.com
georgas@comcast.net

To the seekers of more

Acknowledgements

When I shared with people that I was writing a book about answers to prayer and the miraculous, while some people looked quite uncomfortable about the subject, many others responded with encouragement and excitement. I'm thankful for all the responses, as those are the responses that I will likely have for all of those who glance at this book title. Some will find the whole idea a pile of crap and have zero interest in this subject. But fortunately, many find this subject enticing and exciting, as I do. Thank you to all who believed in my purpose and encouraged me to continue on this journey. I appreciate you more because I know you are a special group of folks.

Having a husband who seems to be able to move mountains through his prayers supplied me with support by his acceptance that these stories are indeed real events by real people and that they all are worth telling. I loved telling him the stories and hearing his faith response to each. He was my listening partner in the story-writing process.

This is the first book I have written that includes the stories of other people. My interviewing and writing process evolved quite a bit between the first person who shared their story and the last. Fortunately, the contributors were patient with me as I figured out this process, which meant going back to them several times for more details, some of which they had to do some digging and pondering to remember. I learned to check back multiple times to be sure they were comfortable with the way their stories were told. Together we partnered to accurately recall and tell these great stories. Thank you to all of the story-sharers for your patience and openness.

As a little girl, my best friend, Mary, told me about Jesus and invited me to attend Sunday school with her. My family wasn't into the church thing, so I was quite curious. I loved going with her, singing happy songs, doing crafts, and learning about God. That started my journey of faith. Mary and I are still close friends today, and she has been a big encourager in the birth of this book, which comes more than fifty years after we first went to church together as little kids.

While all those people are awesome, I am most thankful to God for giving me each of these stories and entrusting me with writing these down. I hope I did them all justice and that in reading them, people will open up their hearts of faith to let God love them more in response.

Table of Contents

Introduction 1

Part I - Healings and Provisions

Listening to God's Leading 7
Perfect Provision 12
Simple Prayer, Miraculous Result 18
Satisfying Love 21
A Word on Fasting 25
Surprise Disappearance 27
New Connections 33
I Can't Do This Anymore 36

Part II - Knowings, Messages and Power from Heaven

A Greeting Card from Heaven 41
Near Miss 47
A Strong Love Conviction 51
The Power of Letting Go 56
A Visit from Heaven 58
Saying Goodbye 60
Custody Miracle 63
He Just Knew 66

Dog Feathers.. 68

Part III - Perseverance, Deliverance, Healing Prayer and Love

"Someone Is Looking out for You" 75
Eyedropper Babies.. 82
Nothing Is Impossible with God.. 84
Love Miracles 88
Too Good To Be True 98
Prayers in the Night 103
Baby Protection 105
Joyful Perseverance 107

Part IV - Divine Direction, God's Humor, Overcoming Evil and Lack of Faith

Not a Secret to God 113
Healing Wounded Hearts.. 118
Paranormal Assault... 127
A Dream Family... 129
Overcoming Fear... 132
God Has a Sense of Humor 135
Unseen Miracles 138

Introduction

Miracle:
An act or event that does not follow the laws of nature and is believed to be caused by God."[1]

- Student's Oxford Canadian Dictionary

I have wanted to write this book for many years. I desired to get down on paper the cool stuff I saw in my own life as answers to prayer. After I wrote my stories, I could see that while those were all great, I didn't have enough to make a full book. I shared this dilemma with a coworker over lunch one day, and she surprised me with, "I've got one for you."

She shared her story, which is in this book now (thank you, Jane). I then realized I needed to ask other people and get their stories too.

That quest turned out to be more challenging than I thought it would be. I thought all people of faith would have a story or two where they saw an answer to prayer that was uncanny. But actually, most did not. Even many of the clergy people I knew didn't have a story for me. At first, I wrongly judged that they lacked faith. But then I remembered that Jesus praised people who believed and hadn't ever seen a

---

[1] "Miracle", *Student's Oxford Canadian Dictionary*, 2nd ed. (Toronto: Oxford University Press, 2007), 674.

miracle. They actually have greater faith. They believe even though they haven't seen someone instantaneously healed or walking on water. And the point of faith isn't to experience miracles. The point of miracles is to experience faith.

I then started asking just about everyone I met, just to see who might have had an encounter with the supernatural of any sort and who was willing to have me write their story for this book. I found the journey of obtaining material very fulfilling. The stories surprised me over and over—both by who had them and how they saw God work in their lives. I found out we are all different in our experiences with God. That opened my heart up to the possibility of new encounters with God, and His miracles.

The point of faith isn't to experience miracles.
The point of miracles is to experience faith.

I hope these stories will do the same for you. That is, I hope we all will open our hearts up to more of God working in our lives in special and powerful ways. I hope we will allow ourselves to believe more is possible, and let God do His cool stuff. And ultimately, I hope it lets us experience God's love for us in very apparent, real, and new ways.

"Blessed are those who have not seen and yet have believed."
—John 20:29, NIV

All of the stories in this book are true; however, a couple of the contributors requested their stories be anonymized. For those accounts, names and/or identifying features were modified to protect identities, but the details of the events that occurred were kept intact.

Part I

Healings and Timely Provisions

Listening to God's Leading

When I pray for a person's healing, my goal is to leave him or her feeling more loved by God than before we prayed.[2]

- John Wimber
  Power Healing

Alexandra Georgas

My friends at the Baptist church where I attended told me about reports of physical healings going on at some of the local churches that were part of the then-new Vineyard denomination. Vineyard was led by John Wimber, founder and former producer of the Righteous Brothers, who turned to a life of faith at twenty-nine and ended up leading this special group of churches. There were many reports of doctor-verified healings going on in the Vineyard churches. My friends and I were interested in learning how to let miracles be part of our lives. We visited these churches together and attended their classes and conferences, eating up the calmly shared, faith-filled words of encouragement.

We went to one of these conferences in Arlington Heights, Illinois. A minister stood up and shared about healing, how it isn't something we have to beg for or get all dramatic

---

[2] John Wimber and Kevin Springer, *Power Healing*, (New York: HarperCollins, 1987), 172.

or emotional over. Just let God. Listen, wait, and let God do what He wants to do. Receive. His manner and message were so refreshingly different than the flamboyant faith healers I had seen on TV.

> Healing isn't something we have to beg for or get all dramatic or emotional over. Just let God. Listen, wait, and let God do what He wants to do.

He ended his talk by saying, "There are some people in this room who are now experiencing tingling in their hands. If that is you, God wants to heal through you." Sure enough, my fingers were strangely tingling. That was weird. He added, "Come on up. We'll have you pray for some people."

I went up to the front of the room, wondering what in the world was this going to be like.

I ended up paired with a young woman. I just gently placed a hand on her arm as I prayed for her. As I prayed, in my mind I saw a Cape Cod–style house, where, as you walk in the front door, you see the stairs right in front of you. To the right is a dining room, and to the left is a living room. I told the woman of the house I was seeing in my mind. She started to sob. Okay. That was weird too. Through the tears she cried, "That's my house."

Apparently, God gave me a vision of her home.

I then saw a husky man walk down the stairs. I told the lady this, and then she really cried. I mean hard sobbing. She finally got out, "That's my dad. That's where he abused me."

Holy moly. Didn't expect that one. I then just prayed for her and for all she went through with him, just saying whatever came to my mind to pray for her. Her sobs turned to weeps, and after about forty-five minutes of me praying for her like this, she was calm and peaceful. I was happy to give this gift to this little lady—a release of her pain. Felt great. And it did feel miraculous that I saw these visions that helped her say what she really needed prayer for and to see the peace she received through my prayers. God worked through me.

How often is God trying to prod me to listen to a voice or inclination from Him, and I just ignore it? I'm guessing all the time. Perhaps we miss the miraculous because we simply ignore it. Miracles could be all around us if we let God do them to us and through us. Time to slow down, listen, and act on those inclinations. We might experience more of God's amazing blessings.

Miracles could be all around us if we let God do them to us and through us.

Alexandra Georgas

"To one there is given through the Spirit a message of wisdom, to another a message of knowledge by means of the same Spirit."
—I Corinthians 12:8, NIV

> To some people this special knowing seems to come in a very special way in the form of definite mental images or verbal impressions; to many of us, however, the knowledge of what to pray for comes in a very natural way, more like a simple intuition.[3]
> - Francis MacNutt
> *Healing*

---

[3] Francis MacNutt, PhD., *Healing* (Notre Dame, Indiana: Ave Maria Press, 1999), 157.

Perfect Provision

We have a God who is infinitely good and who knows what He is doing. He will come and deliver you from your present trouble in His perfect time and when you may least expect it.[4]

- Brother Lawrence
   The Practice of the Presence OF GOD

Anonymous

When they first married, Barry had a habit of drinking a rum and Coke every day after work. His wife, Sally, never drank alcohol and wasn't concerned about Barry's daily habit since he never seemed to be drunk and never went to bars. Barry was a hard worker, contributing much to their daily life by working a full-time job, taking care of the maintenance of their home, and cooking delicious dinners for the family. But as time went on, Barry increasingly showed the effects of a worsening alcohol dependency. Barry's daily drink habit grew to into many more than just one drink. Sally would often find him asleep on the couch early in the evening after having "a drink," which meant he was absent from participating in the family. Sally often tried to talk to Barry and express her concerns, but he always had an ability to talk his way out of the issue.

---

[4] Brother Lawrence, *The Practice of the Presence OF GOD*, (New Kensington, PA, Whitaker House, 1982), 44.

Barry teased Sally often and sometimes the remarks were quite cutting. He often would ridicule the clothes Sally wore as well as put down anything she liked. Sally wanted to hang decorative pictures on their walls, but Barry insisted that everything she liked was ugly, and so their walls were always bare. He also was quite controlling about what she did and who she did things with. However, Sally did not see it as controlling at the time. She accepted his insecure claim that if she really loved him, she would want to stay home all the time with him. Sally wanted to please and love her husband, so she stayed home and became very isolated even though it meant her own needs were neglected.

Sally would try to smooth things over or make things better when Barry would make cutting remarks to the children. When he put them down for not getting higher grades, Sally responded by encouraging her children that what really mattered was that they just do their best.

Over the years, Sally tried talking to Barry about their marriage, but since she didn't think that alcohol was a problem, she only focused on their other marriage issues. Barry rarely acted drunk according to what Sally thought acting drunk should look like. He was very high functioning. He had never been late for work or missed a day of work because of drinking. When she got upset about his actions, he would either apologize, make excuses, or do the bare minimum to make her happy and then go back to his old ways. They also went to a marriage counselor but could only afford three sessions due to lack of insurance coverage.

Some situations were especially difficult to deal with, like when Barry and Sally took their adult daughter out to celebrate her new job. They went to a restaurant that offered a meal with a bottle of wine included. Their daughter didn't like the wine and so didn't drink any. Sally didn't either, as she never drank alcohol. Barry drank the entire bottle himself during their two-hour dinner. Sally was so embarrassed as he stumbled toward the door, needing them to help get him into the car. On the way home, Barry vomited on himself in the back of the car. What should have been a celebration of their daughter's accomplishment was instead all about watching Barry self-destruct in front of everyone. The next day, Barry claimed he had food poisoning and was not sick from the alcohol, although all three had eaten the same food. He scolded Sally for not being more sympathetic to him. He continued to blame others for his problems.

Things became much worse when the company for which Barry worked moved out of state, and he was allowed to work from home full time. Barry's drinking increased. Later he was laid off, and the drinking got even worse. Losing his job was the beginning of the end of their marriage. After that layoff, Barry began indulging early in the day. When they went on a vacation, the first item he put in his suitcase was a bottle of rum. Christmas morning, Sally was surprised to see him pour a rum and Coke as soon as he woke. He also was unmotivated to get a new job and made many excuses about why he couldn't get a job. Sally set him up to get several jobs through friends, which he did take, but then ended up quickly quitting. Sally felt embarrassed. His teasing and cutting remarks increased and became more and more cruel. Arguing became their way of life.

Finally, after one argument, Barry left in the middle of the night. Sally was relieved that he was gone. The next day, she got a phone call from a bail bondsman several states away who reported that Barry was in jail. In a bizarre, spontaneous plan to go visit an old, far-away friend, he had crashed and totaled their car while running from the police. He had open alcohol in the car and was obviously drunk. Barry had reached a new low.

When he came home, Sally hoped that he had reached his rock bottom and that he would truly change this time. Things seemed to be better for a while, but then his behavior became even more bizarre. He started speaking with slurred speech. He even fell asleep at the table trying to eat dinner. Barry had added pain medication to his alcohol dependency. He continued to claim that he wasn't even drinking at all, yet it was quite apparent that he was using heavily.

Sally finally convinced him to go to a counselor again, but his behavior was erratic even in front of the counselor. He was too under the influence to think clearly. At that point, Sally felt like she had exhausted all her options and did not know where else to turn for help. Every time she tried to talk to Barry, he just blamed her for everything. He even tried to blame her for his DUI. The arguing intensified, and Barry was so cruel to Sally that she wondered if he ever loved her. She knew she couldn't take it anymore, so she abruptly left their home.

Sally walked out with only the clothes on her back. Dazed and not really knowing what to do, she went to a hotel. She lay in the hotel bed all night praying nonstop, asking over and over for God's guidance and help. Finally, she prayed, "Dear God, I know we aren't supposed to put the Lord our God to the test, but if you don't find me a place to stay by tomorrow, I am going to take that as a sign that you want me to go back home and live in hell until I die."

The next morning, Sally asked her church friend Alice to go with her to get some clothes from her house. Sally was afraid of what Barry might say or do while she was there packing her things. Alice talked with Barry to help distract him so he wouldn't interfere with Sally's packing. Alice invited Sally to come to her house to talk things over. At Alice's house, the phone rang. The wife of their church's youth group leader called to let them know that someone in the church had a place for Sally to stay. Not only was it a place to stay, but it was for absolutely no charge. Maggie, the women who offered the much-needed shelter, had just recently felt led to open her home to women in crisis. Maggie had gotten divorced several years before and had great compassion for women like Sally.

Sally did go stay with Maggie and found her to be a great support while working through the difficult divorce process. Not only did God answer Sally's prayer for a place to stay on the day she asked for one, but He also gave her a wonderful friendship with Maggie. They are still great friends to this day.

Since that day God has continued to provide for Sally. Even though she has a very modest paying job as a church custodian, she is always able to pay her bills and take care of herself, including keeping and maintaining her home. Unlike when she was married to Barry, she lives debt-free, has been able to save money, and has everything she needs. And she has pictures she loves hanging on her walls. She left that night with literally nothing but since she has seen God provide for her needs over and over again.

"In my distress I called to the Lord, and he answered me."
—Jonah 2:2, NIV

Simple Prayer, Miraculous Result

> Healing sometimes takes place without medicine, through a faith that is important and real.[5]
> - Scott J. Kolbaba, MD
> *Physicians' Untold Stories*

Alexandra Georgas

I was twenty-three years old and still living at home with Dad in Wheaton, Illinois. One night I was lying on my bed saying my prayers to God before going to sleep. I prayed for my best friend, Mary, saying, "Lord please help Mary to get over the bad cold she has." Then I thought, *Hey, I have a sore throat. I should pray for myself.* I then asked God, "Lord, please heal my sore throat too."

Immediately I felt a warmth on the inside of my throat at the top. Slowly it traveled down to the bottom of my throat. It was like Jesus put his fingers on each side of my neck and slowly slid them down, His healing power working within my body as He did.

The warmth was unlike anything I had ever experienced before. The feeling was unlike that of drinking hot tea or the heat from sitting in the sun. It was a gentle, inner warmth.

---

[5] Scott J. Kolbaba, MD, *Physicians' Untold Stories*, (North Charleston, South Carolina, CreateSpace Independent Publishing Platform, 2016), xiii.

My eyes bugged out in disbelief. "Oh, Lord. What? You are healing me?" I asked in amazement. I knew I was experiencing a rare and special miracle. I felt like I was a witness to my body, like a bystander to God working on my physical body.

After the heat reached the bottom of my throat, it dissipated. I responded, "Lord, I don't mean to test you, but I just have to check this."

I swallowed. No sore throat. My eyes welled up in tears. I swallowed again. And again. I just had to be sure. No pain.

I jumped out of bed, got on my knees, and with tears rolling down my cheeks exclaimed, "Thank you God! Thank you so much! Thank you so much, dear Lord! Thank you! Wow!"

I repeated my thanks over and over for a good while. I didn't know what else to say or do but to give Him gratitude.

Why would God give me an instantaneous, miraculous healing of something so minor as a sore throat? That is one of the questions I'll ask Him once I go to Heaven. I don't really know the answer to that question. But I do know that this event changed me. I learned that God can heal people miraculously, and that He cares about all our sufferings, not just major life problems. After this event, I prayed with greater faith, knowing that "with God all things are possible" (Matthew 19:26, NIV). It helped me to ask and ask big. Perhaps that was why God did this. Perhaps the real purpose was to give me an experience that would help me pray more and with more faith. Perhaps that was the greater miracle.

> "If you have faith as small as a mustard seed, you can say to this mountain, 'Move from here to there,' and it will move. Nothing will be impossible for you."
> —Matthew 17:20, NIV

> Noted pollster George Gallop Jr. told me more than twenty years ago that his surveys in the United States revealed that an astounding 7.5 million people reported having received a physical healing in answer to prayer.[6]
> - Pat Robertson
>   *Miracles Can Be Yours Today*

---

[6] Pat Robertson, *Miracles Can Be Yours Today*, (Brentwood, TN: Integrity Publishers, 2006), 144.

Satisfying Love

> The argument up to date shows that miracles are possible and that there is nothing antecedently ridiculous in the stories which say that God has sometimes performed them.[7]
>
> - C. S. Lewis
> *Miracles*

Anonymous

Bob felt sad when his good buddy Andy told him that after twenty-two years, his wife was leaving him. For the first time in their twenty-year friendship, Bob saw Andy cry. Seeing how devastated Andy was after the difficult divorce, Bob felt compassion for his buddy and spent a lot of time just being a good friend to him, listening and giving him company.

    A few years later, Andy introduced Bob to his new girlfriend, June, whom he met at work. June pursued Andy and asked him out over and over until he agreed to see her. She had a petite build with long brown hair and was close to Andy's age. They were playful together and obviously really enjoyed one another.

    Andy later confessed to Bob that June was still married. He was in love with her even so, and he shared that June

---

[7] C. S. Lewis, *Miracles*, (New York: HarperCollins, 1996), 159.

expressed that she loved him. Bob asked Andy, "Why doesn't she leave her husband?"

His only answer was, "It's complicated."

Bob did find out that her husband was wealthy, and they had at least one child together. He imagined the husband sitting in a wheelchair, thinking perhaps that is why she felt obligated to stay with him even though she loved Andy. Bob never did learn more about why she stayed married and still dated his friend.

Andy saw June two times a week, on Wednesday nights and Sunday during the day. Even a neighbor figured out Andy was with a married woman by their rigid schedule. The rest of the week, they had no contact with each other. Bob felt bad that his friend only got to enjoy the woman he loved for such a short time every week. It was like he was accepting crumbs instead of letting himself have a complete meal.

The adulterous affair continued in secrecy for eight years. Then Andy met a new lady, Carrie, who let him know she was interested in him. Desirable Andy was gregarious with a very attractive sense of humor. He decided to give a relationship with Carrie a chance but was still in love with the married woman. He let Carrie know he was seeing someone but that she was married so it wasn't really going anywhere. Carrie wasn't scared away so Andy dated both women at the same time. Bob thought, *Goodness, what a lot of drama!*

Andy was drawn to both women and didn't know which to choose for himself. Bob didn't know either, but his gut told him that the married one was probably not going to be the best path for him. Bob prayed that God would help Andy.

Eventually Andy decided that he loved the married woman and wanted her. He gave her an ultimatum—marry him or they would break up. She finally agreed to marry him. Bob had a sense of dread in his gut at this point. It just didn't seem like the best direction for Andy.

Somehow, she managed to get away from her husband to spend a week on vacation with Andy at his vacation home in Florida. That motivated Bob to increase his prayer intensity for his friend. Bob decided to spend a day both praying and fasting for Andy.

On that very day, Andy and June got into a huge fight, which was so bad that June immediately left and flew back home, abruptly ending the trip, and after eight years, permanently ended the relationship. They never saw each other again after that day of prayer and fasting.

Meanwhile, competitive-natured Carrie was not giving up on the man she wanted. She decided to fly to Florida and fight for Andy. He spent the next week with Carrie, and afterward they continued progressing their relationship. Eventually they married and had a fantastic marriage. She was truly the best woman for Andy. They were married for over thirty years until Andy passed away in Carrie's arms.

God loved Andy even though he was hindering true love in his life by dating a married woman. God heard Bob's prayer and helped to free his friend from that unsatisfying relationship that was going nowhere and then blessed Andy with a woman who gave him the love he really desired, whom he loved deeply as well. After they married, he used to wake up every morning and say, "Thank you God for another day with my wonderful wife. How good you have been to me."

Not only did God save him from a bad relationship and bless him with a great one, He helped Andy see that God loved him. And that was the greatest miracle.

"Whoever turns a sinner from the error of his way will save him from death and cover over a multitude of sins."
—James 5:20, NIV

A Word on Fasting

There is power in prayer and fasting. It is a means of access or entry into the supernatural power of God. Yes, it is God's gateway to spiritual breakthroughs.[8]

- Ronnie Floyd
The Power of Prayer and Fasting

Some of the stories in this book involve prayer with fasting. For people who aren't into the church stuff, that probably sounds very extreme and kind of weird. I get that. But it is an ancient spiritual practice of many religions, and I personally have found it to be very powerful.

But I am pretty wimpy when I fast. I don't think I've ever fasted for an entire day except to get a colonoscopy. I usually skip just one or two meals and, of course, have nothing in between them. I also don't give up any beverages, including coffee. Again, rather wimpy compared to a lot of other more hard-core fasters.

But even so, God has done these miracles in my life with my form of fasting and prayer. Much of the cool stuff I wrote about in this book did happen on those fast days. I still

---

[8] Ronnie Floyd, *The Power of Prayer and Fasting*, (Nashville, TN: B&H Publishing Group, 2010), xiii.

missed food, and when I did, I found myself praying for the requests that were the aim of the fast.

I share this to encourage you to not be too freaked out about the idea of adding fasting to your prayers. Even just a one meal fast where you still drink your favorite coffee drinks can be quite effective. Know that you don't have to be super extreme to see cool stuff when you try fasting. I hope this encourages you to be open to adding fasting prayer into your life so you can enjoy the possibility of seeing God act in even more powerful ways.

> "*So we fasted and petitioned our God about this, and he answered our prayer."*
> *—Ezra 8:23, NIV*
> *Written 399 BC*

Surprise Disappearance

> The most important kind of assertiveness a patient can demonstrate is in the formation of a participatory relationship with the doctor.[9]
>
> - Bernie S. Siegel, MD
> *Love, Medicine & Miracles*

Jane Beal, PhD.

After Jane had moved into her new home in August 2023, she found herself feeling unusually exhausted, which continued for months with no relief. She was experiencing heavy monthly periods, which had become much worse after she had gotten COVID-19 the previous Christmas.

      She went to her doctor for help. Her doctor deducted that this was normal for a woman Jane's age, especially since she had other symptoms that indicated she was going through the perimenopausal stage. She recommended Jane take a progesterone hormonal supplement. But Jane knew that her mother had low iron, which caused exhaustion and had also been the first sign that her mother had cancer. Feeling concerned, Jane asked to be tested to see what her iron levels were. Sure enough, she had low iron. Jane then researched

---

[9] Bernie S. Siegel, MD, *Love, Medicine & Miracles*, (New York: HarperCollins, 1986), 172.

what could be the cause of low iron, and she learned that one reason could be fibroids, which could be one of the causes of her excessive monthly bleeding.

The doctor recommended that she take supplementary iron pills. Jane opted for liquid iron, which is easier on the digestive system. Jane also asked for an ultrasound to see if she might have fibroids that could be causing the bleeding and low iron levels. The doctor agreed. She had two ultrasounds. The first revealed four fibroids external to the uterus. The second revealed a large fibroid tumor right in the middle of Jane's uterus about the size of a grapefruit.

> Fibroid 1: 7.7 x 7.1 x 7.3 cm, central fundus intramural/submucosal

From the Ultrasound report

The doctor then recommended that a biopsy be done on the large tumor inside the uterus. Jane asked if they could just take out the fibroid and biopsy it afterwards instead of doing two procedures. The doctor agreed to try to remove it in a procedure during which Jane was conscious. However, the doctor didn't actually remove the fibroid. Instead, she biopsied a polyp, the tumor, and the endometrial lining of the uterus. This procedure caused pain and complications, so the doctor did not attempt the complete removal of the fibroid while Jane was awake. Instead, she stopped the procedure and scheduled the second one. The plan was for Jane to be put under anesthesia so the large fibroid tumor removal could be completed. Meanwhile, the biopsied material was sent to the lab. It was discovered that Jane had endometrial hyperplasia, which is considered a precancerous condition. Jane met with her doctor who explained that she was at risk of developing atypical cells, which could then develop into uterine cancer. Although only about 5 percent of women with this condition develop cancer from endometrial hyperplasia, Jane was still concerned and so were her doctors.

The doctor again recommended progesterone, which is considered a treatment for endometrial hyperplasia. But Jane had read that one of the side effects of that drug was that it can cause cancer. She discussed this risk with her doctor, who agreed that this was a risk, but stated that it was still the recommended treatment for Jane's condition. Since Jane had such a low risk of cancer at this point, she opted to not begin the hormonal supplement at that time, but rather to wait until her second surgery when the growths in her uterus would be biopsied again. She decided she would keep on asking for prayer for healing at her church and see what God would do for her.

Jane's church has prayer partners available on Sunday mornings to pray for people during the worship service. Every week, Jane went to a prayer partner for prayer for her situation. One week, the woman who prayed for Jane ended the time by saying, "Don't be afraid."

Jane didn't want to be, but that was a struggle. Meanwhile, many people were praying for Jane: her family members, friends, her Bible study group, even one woman who had met her seven years prior was praying continually for Jane, not knowing anything about her health issues.

Jane prayed as well. "Lord, if you want me to go through suffering or cancer for your glory, I will. But if you want me to get healed, let's do it. It's up to you. You can heal me through surgery, or any way you want. May your will be done."

She left it in God's hands. Then oddly, one night she was feeling her belly, but she was not able to feel the large tumor anymore. Previously, she could feel her hard, enlarged uterus all the way up to just below her belly button. It had been the size of a four-to-five month pregnant uterus. No more. Yet she dismissed it, thinking maybe her fibrous uterus had just shifted deeper into her pelvis, and she continued to focus on getting ready for the surgery.

"Lord, if you want me to go through suffering or cancer for your glory, I will. But if you want me to get healed, let's do it. It's up to you. You can heal me through surgery, or any way you want. May your will be done."

The date came for the removal of the fibroids, a surgery called a myomectomy. Jane was scared because she had never been under anesthesia for surgery, and she knew there could be complications. She didn't want to die, she didn't want to hemorrhage, and she didn't want the surgeon to end up having to take out her entire uterus if the fibroid removal went wrong. She just put her trust in God.

After she woke from the sedation, she asked, "Did I make it?"

The nurse reported, "Yes, you did, and you did fine."

After she recovered in the hospital for several hours, she went home.

She later read the surgeon's notes and was shocked to find she had written that she had found a completely normal uterus with no large fibroid found when she went in to do the surgery. It had literally disappeared! Not only was there no large fibroid, but there were also no signs of hyperplasia, as lab analysis confirmed when the doctor sent in a biopsy of part of her endometrium. Fibroids do not typically just go away, and for a grapefruit-sized one to naturally be gone in less than six months is unheard of.

> **Findings:**
> Fairly normal ⋯
> there was no identifiable fibroid.

From the Surgical report

February 14, 2024, Valentine's Day, was the day after the surgery. Jane felt deeply loved by God because He had healed her. She felt as if she was God's special valentine, as we all are.

God loves all of us with love that we can't fully understand. And Jane wouldn't even have known that God had supernaturally healed her unless she had gone through the surgical procedure and the surgeon had reported the miracle to her. How many other times has God given us a miracle, and we don't even know He did it?

Perhaps many more than we would guess.

Alexandra Georgas

How many other times has God given us a miracle, and we don't even know He did it?

"And there was a woman who had had a discharge of blood for twelve years, and who had suffered much under many physicians, and had spent all that she had, and was no better but rather grew worse. She had heard the reports about Jesus and came up behind him in the crowd and touched his garment. For she said," If I touch even his garments, I will be made well." And immediately the flow of blood dried up, and she felt in her body that she was healed of her disease."
—Mark 5:25-29, ESV

Jane Beal, PhD is a tenured, full Professor of English Literature at the University of La Verne, where she specializes in medieval and early modern English literature. She also has worked as a midwife and worked in ministries to help women heal from sexual trauma.

New Connections

Spiritual power is multiplied when more people are praying.[10]

- John Wimber
Power Healing

Bev and Roger Ryan

Nineteen-year-old Roger was unwisely driving too fast as he took a younger intern back to school on his lunch hour. He whipped passed a truck, lost control of his vehicle, and ended up swerving off the road. Roger grabbed the intern with his right arm, pulled him to his side to protect him from the imminent impact, and the car hit a telephone pole at full speed, head-on. Roger's head bounced with great force. Roger was severely injured in the crash. He had a very severe brain stem injury, diagnosed as a detached brain stem. However, not only was the intern unharmed, if Roger hadn't pulled him by his side, the boy's legs would have been broken. But Roger's injury was so substantial that after the initial assessment, the brain specialists were reassigned to other cases because they concluded that Roger would either not live, or if he did, would essentially be in a vegetative state. He was paralyzed from the neck down. The prognosis was dire.

---

[10] John Wimber and Kevin Springer, *Power Healing*, (New York: HarperCollins, 1987), 177.

Roger had been part of a very active, praying church who loved Roger very much and got together frequently to pray. Not only did they pray, but they spread the word to other churches in the area and in other parts of the country, including Roger's grandparents' church. Fervent prayers poured in for Roger.

Roger was in a coma for three months, but then one day he woke, said he was hungry, and asked for a peanut butter sandwich. The medical staff couldn't believe what they were seeing. They interviewed him and determined that he had all his memories up until the accident. They told Roger's mother that the fact his brain was working so well was nothing short of a miracle. They had no medical explanation for how this could be happening. The church community continued to pray. Slowly Roger started gaining more and more of his old self back. The doctors were amazed. They ran scans and discovered that somehow his brain was recircuiting itself around the damaged area. The doctors had never seen anything like this before. His body created new connections that went around the area that was damaged. Again, the doctors reported there was no medical explanation for Roger's recovery.

Roger recovered so fully that he went to school, relearned his trade of welding, got married, and had a son. He is now seventy-five years old, has been married to his wife Bev for forty-seven years, and together they have three beautiful grandchildren, all of whom would not be here today if it weren't for the prayers of the believers and God's great love, mercy, and healing power.

"I tell you that if two of you on earth agree about anything you ask for, it will be done for you by my Father in heaven. For where two or three come together in my name, there I am with them."
—Matthew 18:19-20, NIV

Bev and Roger Ryan are retired and live in Florida near their son, daughter-in-law, and three grandchildren. They enjoy spending their time with the family and the beautiful, warm weather of Florida.

I Can't Do This Anymore

> There is something more than what we can see with our eyes, and prayers are important and may be answered immediately and sometimes in spectacular ways.[11]
>
> - Scott J. Kolbaba, MD
> *Physicians' Untold Stories*

Jane Shu

Jane's little boy was diagnosed with sensory processing disorder when he was only eighteen months old. Grant was extremely sensitive to sound, touch, and strangers. When Jane enrolled him in a local daycare, Grant did not do well. The highly stimulating environment of lively children and activities was very difficult for Grant to process, causing him to cry the whole time he was there.

Conversely, when Grant was a year old, he enjoyed going to a weekend music lesson and was very fond of the teacher, Amy, who led a group of little ones in singing songs and playing games. It was the one place he could enjoy and participate without struggling.

However, at the daycare, Grant continued to suffer and so did Jane. The daycare was going through a period of high turnover, and whenever he started to develop a bond with a

---

[11] Scott J. Kolbaba, MD, *Physicians' Untold Stories*, (North Charleston, South Carolina, CreateSpace Independent Publishing Platform, 2016), xiii.

teacher, that teacher would leave. Grant often struggled, cowering in a corner, crying, and spending each and every day very sad, scared, and upset. During one four-week period, four teachers left. Jane was at the end of her rope. It was so painful to hear the daily report of her little man's terrible struggle and sadness. Finally, on one Monday morning, as Jane drove to drop off her beloved Grant at the day care, she prayed, "God, I need your help to find a solution to this now. I need it today. When I pick up Grant, if he is still upset and crying, I will have to pull him out of the daycare and consider other options."

When Jane arrived that evening to pick up Grant, she saw that he was different. He was calm, smiling, and happy. "Grant had a wonderful day," shared the new teacher.

As the teacher turned around, Jane saw it was Amy, the weekend music teacher who Grant knew and liked and who was so good with Grant. She had started working at the day care center. Amy knew how to work with Grant and help him with his disorder. She was the miraculous answer to Jane's prayers—on the exact day Jane asked for God's help.

In high school Grant ran cross country, was captain of the math team, played trombone in the marching band as well as in the highest auditioned concert and jazz bands, and was in the top two percent of his class. He is currently a sophomore at Yale University.

"Give all you worries and cares to God, because he cares for you."
I Peter 5:7, NLT

Jane Shu is the Director of Data and Analytics at McDonald's Corporation with a Master's degree in Computer Science from Northern Illinois University. She is married with two children, Grant and Annika, enjoys volunteering at Ronald McDonald's Houses and running marathons to raise funds for the charity.

Part II

Knowings, Messages and Power from Heaven

A Greeting Card from Heaven

I'm still learning the mysterious ways in which God moves.[12]

- Francis MacNutt
Healing

Margaret Philbrick

Margaret's mom, Sarah, was an involved grandmother, completely instrumental in raising Margaret's three children. She lived only two miles away, with a key to the house, and Margaret could call on her anytime to help with the kids. Sarah had been a grade-school teacher and applied much of her training with her precious grandchildren. She was also an excellent artist and taught the children to enjoy expressing themselves with drawing, painting, and other art forms. She gave them drawing notebooks and encouraged them to draw how they saw the world, even paying for Art in the Park, a summer drawing camp. She made them do chores but also encouraged them to play. And she made healthy dinners such as baked salmon, teaching the children the value of a nutritious diet. Sarah also loved to garden and taught the kids what was needed to grow a beautiful garden, including pulling lots of

---

[12] Francis MacNutt, PhD., *Healing* (Notre Dame, Indiana: Ave Maria Press, 1999), 116.

weeds and planting bulbs in the autumn. She wanted them to be part of capturing the world around her.

Sarah was also deeply connected to Margaret. They were truly best friends. Every Friday evening Margaret would come over to Sarah's home. They celebrated the end of the week by sipping wine on the back deck, talking about everything and anything.

At the age of eighty-two, Sarah needed to move into an assisted living facility. Even with the excellent care she received, her health continued to decline. Unfortunately, in May of 2020 she was infected with COVID-19 from one of the staff members who was asymptomatic. Nine days after the symptoms manifested, Sarah passed away. Initially, Margaret felt frustrated that someone had brought COVID-19 into the facility, but later let that go, when she realized the person didn't know they were a carrier and there was nothing she could do about it.

The loss of Sarah was nothing short of traumatic for the entire family. The grief hit Margaret's youngest, Nathaniel, especially hard. Margaret put aside her own grief, focusing instead on helping Nathaniel with his intense sadness.

Margaret's Dad was also old and needing a lot of care. Margaret poured her energies into tending to his healthcare needs. Then in January 2023, Margaret's dad passed. At the time of his passing Nathaniel shared the happy news that he and his girlfriend, Amanda, were expecting a baby and decided to also get married. While Margaret was very happy to see her son marry the love of his life and start a family of his own, she found herself missing her mom. Her mom was not there to be a great-grandmother to the new baby as she was to Margaret's kids.

Then Margaret's daughter shared that she and her husband were expecting twins— more mixed emotions. Margaret was so thrilled to have more children to love, but the hole in her heart that her mother left felt even larger. She wished she could ask her mom, "What would you do here? How do we best love twins? How can I be a grandmother like you were with kids and grandkids in different states?"

Margaret started dreaming about her mother and talking to her. "Mom, I miss you. I'm going to be a grandmother now. I wish I could ask you how you did it, but I'm just going to have to draw on whatever lessons you gave to me with my kids." She wondered, *Can Mom hear me? Am I just talking to myself?*

Margaret and her husband Charlie rented a home in the Nashville area near Nathaniel and Amanda, so that they could help with their soon-to-be born grandson. She helped them get the baby room ready in an adorable dinosaur theme. Margaret thoroughly enjoyed buying T-Rex decorations for the new child on the way. It was a fun and joyous time.

Little Asher was born in the summer, and Margaret found herself full of natural flowing grandmotherly love. She discovered a beautiful green space nearby and decided one of her new traditions would be to take little baby Asher on strolls. Crooked Branch Park is an extremely well maintained, beautiful park with a lovely river. Margaret would point out to Asher sights along the way. "See the pretty purple flowers, Asher?

That's a butterfly bush." "Hear that bird call? That's a cardinal. It has a bright red color, doesn't it?"

Margaret would also pray as she strolled. One day in September 2023 as she was walking, she prayed, "Gosh, Lord, I just miss my mother. I know that she is with you in Heaven, but I guess I would like to just have a sense that she sees what we are doing and that we are doing the right thing."

She then turned a corner and saw a cottonwood tree spreading its cottony leaves all over the pavement. It reminded her of when her oldest son used to run cross-country, and she would bike alongside him. "Asher, your Uncle Caleb used to run and run, and the paths would be covered in cottonwood leaves just like this."

Just then she looked down and saw a tiny piece of paper. It was half of a card that one might use with a bouquet of flowers. This was a very unusual occurrence, since Margaret had been walking in this park for months and there was never anything but leaves and butterflies, not a speck of paper or trash of any sort. Margaret picked it up and saw on one side it had a cute little dinosaur picture and read, "Surprise!" She flipped over to the other side and read, "Love, Mom."

Margaret stopped dead in her tracks. Tears welled up in her eyes. She knew this was an answer to her prayer. It was like her mom was saying, "I see everything you are doing. I saw you buy all those cute dinosaur items for the nursery. I see you strolling with Asher now. I am still with you."

Margaret found herself deeply comforted. Her Mom was still with her.

Margaret is treasuring all her time with all her grandchildren and hoping to be the kind of grandmother her mom was to her children. Margaret is now writing letters to Asher each time they stroll through Crooked Branch Park, telling him all the things they shared and saw, including the incredible little surprise visit from his great-grandmother.

"To him who alone does great wonders, His love endures forever."
—Psalm 136:4, NIV

Margaret Ann Philbrick is an author, gardener, teacher, wife, mom, and new grandma. She loves digging in the dirt and helping new works grow and flourish; and that includes children, churches, plants, trees, poems, and stories. You can find her writing on the road somewhere among Wisconsin; Saint Louis, Missouri; and Nashville, Tennessee, where her family lives. When not on the road, she is likely in a forest.

Near Miss

> When we feel something nudging us, we need to listen.
> This is one way that God speaks to us.[13]
> - Doug Fyckes
> *Modern Day Miracles*

Becky

After visiting his parents in Missouri, Drew, Mom and Dad were heading to Colorado where Drew lived. Mom and Dad were going to visit Colorado for the first time. Drew's mother, Becky, was working that day, so they started the twelve-hour drive after she finished with her work, giving them a late start. Drew had flown to Missouri, but they were driving back together instead of all flying and so they needed to pick up Drew's vehicle from Denver Airport on the way to Drew's home. The drive from the airport in Denver to Drew's home in Colorado Springs was about 1.5 hours. Drew would then lead the way for the final leg of the trip, with his parents following. Becky was driving Mom and Dad's car. Needless to say, it was very late by the time they picked up the vehicle, and they still had another 1.5-hour drive left. Everyone was exhausted.

The drive was uneventful until they were about twenty miles from Drew's home. Unexpectedly, Drew pulled over into a rest stop. He felt strongly that his parents needed to switch

---

[13] Doug Fyckes and Allison C. Restagno, *Modern Day Miracles* (Shippensburg, PA: Destiny Imager, Publishers, 2011), 71.

drivers. Mind you, it was around 3 a.m., and they were only twenty minutes away from Drew's home. Becky was frustrated that they were stopping.

"Why are you stopping?" Becky complained. "I just want to be done."

"I felt you needed to switch drivers," Drew explained.

"I'm fine!" Becky responded tersely. "We don't need to stop here. We are almost done. Why did you think we needed to switch drivers?"

"I don't know," Drew said. "I just felt you needed to switch. Maybe you were tired? I just felt Dad needed to drive."

"What are you talking about?" Becky asked.

"Sorry," Drew apologized for frustrating his mom. "I really felt you needed to switch."

Becky's frustration was high, but she went ahead and switched drivers. They commenced the last stretch of the drive, the final twenty miles home. However, they only drove for about another minute before they came upon a multi-car accident with two semi-trucks, two pickup trucks, and two cars. One of the trucks looked like it had been sawed in half. It was a bad wreck, and it was fresh, with no emergency personnel on site yet. Worse, these were the same vehicles that they were driving near, right before pulling off the road at the rest stop. Had they not pulled over, there is a good chance that their vehicles would have been involved in the large collision. Becky's frustration immediately evaporated. The unexpected act of switching drivers in the middle of the night, right before arriving at the destination, likely avoided joining a multi-car pileup.

At Drew's house he told his parents, "I just had a very strong urging that we had to stop for you two to switch drivers."

Becky apologized for complaining and thanked him for trusting his strong inner prodding. She also thanked God they all arrived safe and without being part of an accident.

Becky wonders how many other times God protected them that she wasn't aware of. Probably many more than she realizes. Probably way more than any of us realize.

Drew and Becky

And the angel of God, which went before the camp of Israel, removed and went behind them; and the pillar of the cloud went from before their face, and stood behind them: And it came between the camp of the Egyptians and the camp of Israel; and it was a cloud and darkness to them, but it gave light by night to these: so that the one came not near the other all the night.
—Exodus 14:19-20, KJV

Becky has been married to her husband Patrick since 1979 and together they have three sons and eight grandchildren. She worked for 35 years mostly with special education children and adults, developing programs and materials that were used in schools, day care centers, and other facilities for special needs children. She currently is semi-retired, working part time at her church, Praise Assembly in Springfield Missouri, as a Facilities Use Coordinator. She also volunteers through her church in a number of ministries, including helping their prison ministries, providing assistance to domestic violence victims, veterans and the homeless.

A Strong Love Conviction

> We have the choice to use the gift of our life to make the world a better place—or not to bother.[14]
>
> - Jane Goodall

Alexandra Georgas

My husband, Don, had just started a new job as a laborer for Muehfelt Enterprises in Wheaton, Illinois, a plumbing, excavation, sewer, and water installation and repair business. The owner and boss was Karl Muehfelt.

One winter day Karl's daughter got into a car accident that she mistakenly caused, sliding into a ditch. The work crew, including my husband, drove with Karl to the scene of the accident to help retrieve the car. As Don shared the story with me that evening, I expected to hear about how Karl scolded his daughter for her mistake, which is usually what I got from my dad when I caused a car accident a few times in my youth. But no, without saying a word, Karl just walked up to his daughter and held her. No reprimand, no scold, just comfort.

Karl's calm and wise fatherly love moved me. "That's a special guy," I reflected to Don.

---

[14] Jane Goodall, Peggy Anderson, *Great Quotes from Great Women*, (Naperville, Illinois: Simple Truths, 2017) 63.

And surprisingly, I had the idea come into my head that Karl might be a good guy for my therapist friend, Annie. I told Don of my connection idea and asked him, "Find out if Karl is married."

My reluctant husband laughed and asked, "How am I supposed to do that? He's a very quiet guy, barely says anything."

I said, "That's easy, just ask the women in the office. They'll tell you."

Don did find out from the women that Karl was divorced and reported his findings to me.

"Great," I said. "Now let me find out from Annie if she is interested before we ask Karl."

Don was relieved that at least at that point he was off the hook. Don had worked for Karl for only a few months and didn't know him that well. He was hoping Annie would say she was not interested, and we could drop the whole crazy idea.

The next time I saw my friend Annie, I surprised her by declaring, "Annie, I have someone who might be a good person for you. I think that you and Don's new boss might get along. Would you be interested in meeting him?"

Annie sure didn't see that coming. "I don't know," she said. "Tell me about him."

I told her the story of the daughter and the car accident. "What does he wear?" she asked.

"He's pretty tall, thin, and he usually wears khakis and a button-down shirt."

I guess that did it because Annie then handed me not one, but three of her business cards pressed together and said, "Sure, I'll meet him."

I ran home and told my dear husband that Annie was willing to meet Karl. I had an unusual and strong inner conviction that this needed to happen. I pushed poor Don hard, and he reluctantly agreed to ask the boss about the idea.

The next day he managed to utter the words to his new boss, "Are you seeing anybody these days?"

Karl answered, "No," followed by a silence.

Don had a celebration in his heart thinking he did his job to ask and now it was over. But then Karl added, "Why, do you have someone in mind?"

Don thought to himself, *Oh, crap. Now I have to ask him.* He forced out the words, "Yeah, my wife has a friend of hers that she thinks you might like. Here are her business cards." He handed Karl all three. "She is a therapist, but I'm not saying you need one."

Karl laughed and confessed, "We all can use a therapist!"

Karl and Annie, with many back and forth efforts to connect, talked on the phone for an hour on a Saturday afternoon in February. For their first date, they met at a local IHOP for Sunday brunch after they each went to their respective churches. They again talked for nearly six hours.

I knew Karl would like Annie, as Annie is the most loving, wise, incredible person I've ever known. She would also ascertain quickly whether Karl would be a good person for her to date. I had the conviction that if Annie liked Karl, then they would marry. It was weird to be so sure with so little data.

I asked Annie after their first date what she thought of Karl. She replied, "I like him. He is so nice!" And she went on to describe the good she saw in him.

I then told her, "You're going to marry him."

She looked stunned and responded incredulously, "What? You think so, huh?"

I stayed quiet. I figured she'd find out in time. But in my heart I knew they would marry.

Annie did come to know only six weeks later that this was the man for her. God showed her very clearly. God must have been working in Karl's heart as well. On a Sunday afternoon walk where they held hands for the first time, Karl brought up the hope he had for marriage with Annie. This conversation and consideration of God's plan happened before they had even kissed! They did marry one-and-a-half years later and continue having good long conversations to this day.

I have tried over and over since then to recreate this magical matchmaking, but for almost all of my subsequent attempts, they flopped after the first date. These love failures have confirmed to me that it was God leading me in matchmaking Karl and Annie and that I was just a vessel to get it all started. God was the matchmaker, not me. God just gave me an uncanny conviction that was so strong I knew it was His plan. I'm so glad I listened to that inner prodding and that Don listened to me. We got to help God create a new family. What a great gift that is!

> *"[A]nd after the fire, a still small voice."*
> —I Kings 19:12, KJV

Karl and Annie

The Power of Letting Go

> The Bible gives me a deep, comforting sense that things seen are temporal, and things unseen are eternal.[15]
>
> - Helen Keller

Todd Niewold

Todd's mother, Elaine, suffered with declining dementia for three years, after having a number of strokes. She was in the late stages of the illness and under hospice care in a nursing home. The strokes took away her ability to talk or write, adding another layer of emotional isolation for her. Watching the expressions of confusion and pain on her beautiful, wrinkled face was deeply painful for the family. They loved her so much and felt so sad to see her suffering. Finally, one day Todd was in church and found himself praying, "Lord, please take her." He had never asked for anything like this before in his life, and even felt guilty saying the words.

After church he went to visit his dear mother in the nursing home. When he arrived, the staff told him that during that very hour he was in church his mom did pass away, right as Todd prayed that releasing prayer.

Todd struggled with guilt knowing he had asked for God to take her. But he was comforted by the belief that it was truly

---

[15] Helen Keller, Peggy Anderson, *Great Quotes from Great Women*, (Naperville, Illinois: Simple Truths, 2017), 84.

a blessing for her to be freed from her failing body and to enter into the full presence of God's love in Heaven. Todd's prayer was a prayer of selfless love, and he knows that God would not have taken her if it wasn't the best path of love for his mother.

"And God shall wipe away all tears from their eyes; and there shall be no more death, neither sorrow, nor crying, neither shall there be any more pain: for the former things are passed away."
—*Revelation 21:4, KJV*

Todd Niewold is a retired police officer who has been married to his wife for forty-two years. He enjoys bowling, being Santa at Christmas time, but most of all, spending as much time as possible with his adorable grandchildren.

A Visit from Heaven

> The love that exists between family members is one of the strongest forces in the universe.[16]
>
> - Scott J Kolbaba, MD
>   *Physicians' Untold Stories*

Anne Baron

In 2004, Anne had major surgery to remove scar tissue that was causing her celiac artery to be compressed. The surgery was so extensive that the surgeon had to put sixty-five staples in her midriff area. Anne did not respond well to the operation, and the doctors were very concerned that she would not live through the night. Anne was sleeping in the hospital bed when she felt someone grab ahold of her foot and shake it. She woke, looked to see who it was and saw her father standing there at the foot of her bed rubbing her foot. She recognized him with his familiar glasses, shirt, pants, and gym shoes.

He said to her, "You're going to be okay. We aren't ready for you."

She couldn't believe it because her father had passed away fifteen years earlier, but there he was standing in her

---

[16] Scott J. Kolbaba, MD, *Physicians' Untold Stories*, (North Charleston, South Carolina, CreateSpace Independent Publishing Platform, 2016), 142.

room, rubbing her feet, and talking to her. Anne then fell back to sleep and rested peacefully.

The next day, there was an unexpected and marked change in Anne's condition. She was surprisingly much better. She was able to walk unassisted for the first time since the surgery. All her vitals showed a noticeable change for the better. She was later released and has lived many years since that time.

Anne and Dad

"And there appeared before them Elijah and Moses, who were talking with Jesus."
Mark 9:4, NIV

Anne Baron has worked as a hair stylist for fifty-three years. She has a devoted partner, Bruce, two daughters, four grandchildren, many great friends, and her beloved dog, Roger.

Saying Goodbye

Alexandra Georgas

When I was twenty-four years old, I dated John, a divorced army vet with a young daughter living in France with her mother. He was staying in his brother's basement, working on rebuilding his life. We had a fun case of mutual infatuation.

After a few months of dating, I decided to end the relationship. John had confessed to me that he had hit his ex-wife, and I could see he was struggling with alcoholism. He was also overly possessive and jealous of me, all signs to me that he had more healing to do before he was ready for healthy, long-term love.

I hadn't dated that much even by that age, and I was not very assertive. So I ended it by saying, "I think we should take a break" rather than what I really wanted to say, which was that we were done and I was moving on.

About six months later, John sent a dozen long-stem red roses to me to my office at work. I was not flattered. A wave of apprehension came over me.

To make matters worse, a few days after that, I was driving home from work when I could see his face in my rear-view mirror as he was following me in his car. That really freaked me out. I felt threatened and like he had stalked me. This was not okay with me.

On a day soon after that, I decided to fast and pray about the situation, going without food from the time I rose until the time I picked for the fast to end, which was 4:00 p.m. I was shocked when at precisely 4:00 p.m. my phone rang, and it was John. I hadn't spoken to him for six months, and he called me at the exact time my fast ended. He wanted us to start dating again. Emboldened with my day of prayer and still shaken from his stalking, I was able to say to him with much more clarity and strength, "No, John. I am not interested in that. We each need to move on."

He was surprised at my firm directness. But that worked. I never talked to him or saw him again after that conversation. God gave me the strength and opportunity to tell him what needed to be stated. I hope he did work on himself and that he found a better life. But he was not a safe person for me. I'm thankful God helped me be free to go forward in a healthier path. And I did.

Later that week, I found out that my great-grandmother passed away on the very day I fasted: February 4, 1985. She and I had been quite connected. Over the years, we had written each other many letters and I visited her several times in her later years. She had had trouble in her life when it came to marriage, although the family has heard different versions of her story, so we aren't entirely sure which of her two husbands were worse. We know she seemed to be running around the country with her second husband. One story was that he was still married to his first wife. Was there a connection between me and my great-grandmother on that day? Does a person get to make a pit stop before going to Heaven? I wonder if she said, "Hey, Lord, I need to go give strength to my great granddaughter before I leave Earth. I don't want her to make the same mistakes I made." And did she somehow visit me and help me be empowered? I have no idea, but it is kind of fun to think about. I guess I'll ask about that when I go to Heaven.

I married years later a man who was safe, steady, caring, kind, and just wonderful. He was the best man for me.

"[Y]e have not because ye ask not."
—James 4:2, KJV

Custody Miracle

Alexandra Georgas

At age thirty-six, I joined a cheap dating service, and for the fifty-dollar fee, I was set up with a divorced man with shoulder-length brown hair who had the most caring eyes I had ever seen in a man. Less than two years later, I found myself at the altar, exchanging vows and singing a love song I wrote to him. Along with him, I received the honor of loving his three kids and, later, our two precious grandchildren. Certainly, that was the best fifty bucks I ever spent!

After we first met, Don had told me that his two younger teenage children were living with his ex-wife, who had unmedicated bipolar disorder and was an alcoholic. We learned later she was also using drugs. I told Don how deeply disturbing it was for me when I was a teenager and lived with a mom with an untreated mental illness. I told him he had to get them out of that situation, and that it was probably much worse than he feared. Don believed me, but he didn't have any proof of grounds for obtaining custody of the children.

We joined together in prayer. Our first answer came one day when his ex called him out of the blue and declared, "I can't take our daughter anymore. You take her!"

And—poof—Don's daughter, Kristyn, came to live with Don, just like that. We thought Don's ex could have been attempting to scare me away from marrying him, because the incident occurred soon after we became engaged. But having Kristyn live with her father was exactly what Don and I earnestly wanted. However, Don didn't have legal custody yet, and his youngest child, Danny, was still living with his mother.

On the following Monday, we decided to both fast and pray for two meals, during breakfast and lunch until 4:00 p.m., asking God to somehow work it out so Don could gain permanent custody of both Kristyn and Danny. At the end of our fast on that very day, Don got a call during which he learned that his ex-wife, who practiced witchcraft, had tried to cast a spell, which involved igniting a stack of Bibles and burning a pentagon into the kitchen floor. She then slit her wrists. She had started the indoor fire while Danny was sleeping in the next room, risking his life. She was checked into the psychiatric ward of the local hospital, and Danny went to live with Don that same day.

The temporary custody hearing two weeks later lasted five minutes. Don's lawyer reported that it was the fastest custody hearing he'd ever witnessed. The permanent custody hearing a month later lasted less than a half hour. Don had all the evidence he needed to gain full custody, and his ex-wife had no sensible rebuttal.

After Don and I married, the adjustment was difficult for all of us. Some women wouldn't have taken on teenage stepkids, but I had prayed for it and was happy to be their stepmom, even if they weren't so sure about me. I knew firsthand what they had lived through, and I knew Don and I had to do all in our power to help them. And so we did. Because of what I had gone through in my own life, I was open to welcoming teens into my life, loving them, and making them my own family. God released his mercy on all of us.

"But if any of you causes one of these little ones who trusts in me to lose his faith, it would be better for you to have a rock tied to your neck and be thrown into the sea."
—Matthew 18:6, TLB

He Just Knew

JJ and Kristy Johnson

Kristy's mother, Ella, was diagnosed with a non-malignant tumor on the pituitary gland. The pituitary gland is the master gland of the endocrine system which controls many hormone glands in the body. The whole family had many concerns about what this could mean.

Kristy's husband, JJ, was very close to Ella. His mother-in-law had become one of his closest friends. JJ always said that mother-in-law jokes never applied to Ella. He cherished her and their time around cups of coffee and Hardee's biscuits. The possibility of losing her weighed heavily on JJ's heart.

JJ was away in Ohio on one of his long-haul trips as a truck driver. As he drove and prayed, a strong feeling came over him, which gave him the inner conviction that Ella was going to be all right and survive this. He somehow just knew.

When he returned home, Kristy reported that her mother had another brain scan, and to everyone's surprise and relief, the tumor had shrunk! The doctors had no logical explanation for this change. JJ was ecstatic, as this news absolutely confirmed the overwhelming sense of peace he had received while he was praying. Kristy and JJ both knew then that Ella was going to be all right.

No surgery was necessary, and Ella lived for another sixteen years with the dormant, shrunken, non-malignant tumor on the pituitary gland causing no ill effects.

JJ and Ella returned to drinking coffee and eating biscuits at Hardee's giving thanks and credit to God for her healing.

"Now faith is the assurance of things hoped for, the conviction of things not seen."
—Hebrews 11:1, ESV

JJ has worked as an over-the-road truck driver for forty-three years. He has been married to his wife, Kristy, for thirty-nine years. They are actively involved in their church, Grace Presbyterian located in Peoria, Illinois.

Dog Feathers

> I'm sort of in love with what I don't know. I'm in awe of what is not explainable or predictable.[17]
>
> - Meryl Streep

Sue Todd

Susan was delighted when she found an adorable little Shih Tzu dog at the shelter. She gave her three-year-old fur baby the name of Crissy and from the beginning, the two were inseparable. Susan brought Crissy with her wherever she went, on trips, to the grocery store, out to dinner, everywhere. She treated Crissy more as her child than a pet. She never gave her dog food but made special meals for her precious companion of scrambled eggs, rice, chicken, homemade dog biscuits, and other treats. She even made a little stroller for her fur daughter so that she could roll her to the car and Crissy would not burn her little feet on the hot Arizona pavement. Nothing was too

Susan and Crissy

---

[17] Meryl Streep, Peggy Anderson, *Great Quotes from Great Women*, (Naperville, Illinois: Simple Truths, 2017), 207.

good for her best buddy. Crissy brought Susan incredible joy and love, and Susan gave Crissy great devoted love as well.

Dogs are miracles with paws.[18]
- Susan Kennedy

After fourteen years together, little Crissy's health failed terribly. Susan knew the kind act was to end her suffering. Susan warned her daughters, "I'm not going to live long without her."

Crissy in her stroller

But she made the sacrifice to end Crissy's suffering at seventeen years old. She told her daughters that when she passed, she wanted her ashes combined with little Crissy's. The girls heartily agreed, knowing how much their mom loved their adopted fur sister.

Susan missed Crissy deeply.

One day as she was outside in her yard she found a single white feather next to her shoe. She thought that was very strange since it just appeared out of nowhere. She picked up the little feather and wondered what it meant.

---

[18] Susan Kennedy, Amy Newmark, *Chicken Soup for the Soup: Miracles & Divine Intervention*, (Cos Cob, Connecticut: Chicken Soup for the Soul, 2021), 56.

On another day she sat down on a lawn chair in her back yard and to her surprise, saw a little white feather sitting on the cushion on the chair right next to her. She felt in her heart that somehow this was a sign that her little Crissy's love was still with her. She felt comforted by the tangible gift.

This strange phenomenon of a white feather appearing out of nowhere kept reoccurring for Susan whenever she missed Crissy. She would then find a new little white feather over and over. The signs were a great comfort for her and helped her with her grief; although, even two years after Crissy passed, Susan found herself crying from time to time, missing her best friend. She kept finding these feathers at her feet or side whenever she missed her little dog.

Then Susan had a stroke at ninety-four years old. Susan's two out-of-state daughters, Sue and Nancy, came into town to tend to their mother along with her other local daughter, Debbie. The family honored Susan's wishes by placing her into a hospice facility. Only five days after the stroke, Susan passed away.

Susan's family was surprised their mom passed so fast but comforted that she didn't suffer long. But they were sad. They missed her, but they were all together staying at Debbie's home, which was a comfort.

Debbie's husband went to Susan's house to gather Crissy's ashes, the special plaque Susan had made to remember Crissy by, along with some of her belongings. He put the plaque and ashes on the dining room table, and everyone went to bed.

In the morning when Debbie passed by the dining room table, she noticed a little white feather on the table. Debbie asked the others, "Where did that come from?" and pointed to a little white feather between Crissy's ashes and the memorable plaque.

The others all replied, "What feather?"

Everyone then saw the little feather and found the hairs on their arms standing up. They all believed it was a sign from their mom that she was still with them and loving them.

A few days later, the sisters went to their mother's home. And as soon as Sue stepped out of her car, there was a little white feather next to her foot, just like the one on the dining room table. Sue smiled big, feeling the presence of her mother's love by this peculiar and special little sign.

Since Susan's passing, whenever Sue or Debbie were thinking about their mother, a new little white feather would appear.

These peculiar little white feathers have been beautiful comforting tokens to the ladies of this family, that those they loved somehow still love them from afar and they are never really alone.

"For all things are possible with God."
—*Mark 10:27, ESV*

Sue Todd and her husband own an electrical equipment manufacturing company, have three children and ten grandchildren. Sue loves making cards by hand, scrapbooking, sewing, and enjoying time with family and friends.

Part III

Perseverance, Deliverance, Healing Prayer and Love

"Someone Is Looking out for You"

You will never truly know yourself, or the strength of your relationships, until both have been tested by adversity.[19]

- J. K. Rowling

Lola Moore

In 1991, Lola found a lump on her neck about the size of an almond. She showed it to a nurse friend who encouraged her to go to her doctor as soon as possible to get it checked out. She did, and the doctor shared that it was a swollen lymph node and ordered a chest x-ray. The x-ray showed that Lola had a large mass in her chest, covering about 64 percent of her chest area. It was inoperable.

The doctors diagnosed it as Hodgkin's Lymphoma. Lola then went through ten months of weekly chemotherapy, starting in November 1991. One Sunday during treatment, she told her husband, Michael, "I want to go to church."

He asked, "Are you sure? You are so tired and weak."

Lola assured, "If I can go to get chemo tomorrow, I can go to church today. I want to go to church."

It was winter, and she was very frail, so her husband wrapped her in loads of layers, to the point she looked a bit

---

[19] J. K. Rowling, Peggy Anderson, *Great Quotes from Great Women*, (Naperville, Illinois: Simple Truths, 2017), 180.

like the Pillsbury Doughboy. She sat in the back and worshipped. She kept going to church weekly even though she was quite worn out from the chemo.

When she first received treatment, she got very sick and vomited quite a bit. Then, in her second month of treatment, Zofran, a new anti-nausea drug came out, which did the job well in keeping Lola from being nauseous from the chemo. But Lola did lose all her hair like many chemo patients. Her pigment was gray, and her weight ballooned as well.

The chemo took a huge toll on her overall health, and in January she was hospitalized for a month. By the end of January, her red blood cell count dropped dangerously low, and she had a 105-degree fever. The doctors diagnosed her with interstitial pneumonia, which is a form that causes inflammation in the structural space of the lungs. The life expectancy of someone with interstitial pneumonia is three to five years. The chemo drug was attacking the lining of her lung.

Lola kept praying in the hospital, "Lord, please don't let me die. Michael needs me." Michael had already lost his parents together in a car accident, and Lola and Michael did not have children. Lola's heart cried out for Michael to not have another devastating loss of losing his wife. Lola tried not to sleep in the hospital because she was afraid she wouldn't wake up and would leave Michael alone.

The doctors told her she needed a blood transfusion. At first Lola refused because at the time there were many stories of people getting AIDS from blood transfusions. Her red blood cell count continued to decline so she finally agreed. Once it was completed, she felt like a new woman. Color returned to her skin, and she felt much more alive. God answered her prayers and kept her alive long enough to get the transfusion she needed.

The ten months of chemo reduced the tumor to the size of a dime. She then began sixteen weeks of radiation on the remaining tumor. The doctors warned that patients like her often find themselves battling other cancers later. Heart and lung issues also often present themselves years after chemotherapy treatments.

Eighteen years later, a lump was discovered in Lola's right breast, which the doctors wanted to check out. The results were that Lola had breast cancer. She had a double mastectomy. Fortunately, Lola has been cancer-free since 2010.

But she has not been trouble-free. On September 11, 2023, Lola decided to walk the short distance to their local bank to pick up Euros. On September 18, Michael and Lola were leaving for a month to hike in Italy and Greece. She found she had to rest after only walking two blocks, which never happened to her before. She managed to get to the bank and back, resting after every couple of blocks. Later that evening after dinner, Michael found Lola blacked out on the kitchen floor. He was able to revive her, calling her name and helping her up into a chair, and they immediately went to the emergency room.

The doctors ran many tests and could not find anything wrong. The cardiologist concluded that she was just dehydrated. But Lola knew that was very unlikely since she drinks at least a half gallon of water a day. Lola is only four foot nine inches tall and weighs 113 pounds. Her intuition was telling her there was something wrong with her heart. She reminded the doctor that every time they tested her heart she was lying down and resting. She asked for a stress test to see what was really going on. The doctor refused, saying it was not necessary and continued creating the order for her release. Lola boldly declared, "See those gym shoes sitting there on the floor? I'm not putting them on unless it's for a stress test. And I'm not leaving the hospital until you give me one."

The doctor left the room. Lola's nurse came in and asked why she was crying. Lola explained she felt something was wrong and wanted to have a stress test. Her nurse, Lynn, left and returned shortly with two administrative employees. They asked many questions and said they would consult and return with a decision. They agreed that against the doctor's decision, Lola would go down to the lab for a stress test.

Six minutes into the stress test Lola was "Code Blue." Her heart completely stopped. Fortunately, Lola came to just as they were about to use the paddles.

Meanwhile, Michael was in the family waiting room when he heard over the intercom system the "Code Blue" announcement. He then went into the adjacent chapel to pray for the person near death's door. Little did he know that he was praying for his wife.

A new cardiologist got involved and told Lola the electrical function of her heart was nearly completely disconnected, and she was hanging on by a thread. The only option was immediate surgery for a pacemaker. He also added, "For your heart to stop twice in less than twenty-four hours, and for you to still be here, well, someone must be watching over you."

He also warned that since Lola was so tiny and had previous breast cancer surgeries this would be difficult to position. However, a representative from the company that makes the pacemakers "happened" to be at that hospital that day and agreed to assist with the surgery. It was put in successfully with no issues.

When Lola fell on her kitchen floor, she fell full force on her chest. There was a concern that perhaps one of her breast implants might have ruptured from the impact. An MRI was required to diagnose a rupture. Due to the newly placed pacemaker, she could not have the MRI for eight weeks because she wasn't allowed to put her arms above her head. Ruptured implants can lead to silicon poisoning, which was a major concern. There was nothing Lola could do but wait and pray.

After eight weeks, she had the MRI, and they found that one of the implants had ruptured. Miraculously the silicone gel did not spread anywhere as the scar tissue from her previous surgeries held the gel in place like a dam. Lola had hated the painful scar tissue for twelve years, and now it had saved her life. Then to her great surprise, her breast surgeon commented, "Someone must be watching over you."

The next bad news was that while the doctor reported the breast implants had to come out as soon as possible, there wasn't an opening for the surgery for four months. Lola's heart sank. The nurse walked out of the room but returned a few minutes later. "Good news, someone just cancelled for next month."

Lola was so relieved. Surgery was scheduled for December 8, which was Michael's mom's birthday. God was watching over her once again.

> Never lose hope. Just when you think it's over...
> God sends you a miracle.[20]
> - Author Unknown

Lola had the surgery and is doing great recovering from everything, both physically and emotionally. The reality that she was on the edge of death so many times has settled in, and she is comforted that over and over she kept hearing doctors say, "Someone is watching over you."

Not all doctors are right about all things, but they were right about that. God is looking over her and she knows it more than ever.

> *"But seek first his kingdom and his righteousness, and all these things will be given to you as well."*
> —Matthew 6:33, NIV

---

[20] Amy Newmark, *Chicken Soup for the Soup: Miracles & Divine Intervention*, (Cos Cob, Connecticut: Chicken Soup for the Soul, 2021), 24.

Lola Moore is retired from forty-seven years of working in the field of dentistry. She enjoys volunteering for her church and at the local food pantry. She also enjoys opera, ballet, cooking, baking, and hiking throughout the United States, Canada, and Europe. She and her husband Michael have been married since 1981 and attend Old St. Patrick's Catholic Church in Chicago, Illinois.

Lola and Michael
December 2023
Three weeks after breast surgery

Eyedropper Babies

> I believe that all of us have the potential for being used in healing.[21]
>
> - Francis MacNutt
> *Healing*

Veneta and Alexandra Georgas

My Dad, Alex, and his twin brother, Tom, were born on August 28, 1933. They were tiny premature babies—so small, Grandma had to feed them with an eye dropper. In Greek tradition, the first-born male is named after the father's father. But these tiny ones were not expected to live. So, my grandparents named them after famous Greek conquerors instead, Alexander the Great and General Themistocles.

The babies were not doing well. The Greek Orthodox priest came over to the house, anointed the twins with oil, and prayed over them. Grandma shared with me on many occasions how after that anointed prayer her little babies got better. She believed the priest's prayer released the healing her boys needed and saved their little lives.

Both Dad and Uncle Tom lived to be old men, after marrying and creating more generations of children, including myself. I would likely not be here today if not for that priest's

---

[21] Francis MacNutt, PhD., *Healing* (Notre Dame, Indiana: Ave Maria Press, 1999), 243.

prayer of faith. One man's miraculous prayer gave us generations of family.

"Is anyone among you sick? Let him call for the elders of the church, and let them pray over him, anointing him with oil in the name of the Lord."
—*James 5:14-15, ESV*

Veneta Vlagopoulou Georgas immigrated from Greece in 1922 when she was twenty-four years old. She worked as a nanny and housekeeper for her uncle, John Raklios, and his wife, Mary, until she married Theodore Georgas in 1928. They had a daughter Connie, twin boys, and six grandchildren. She enjoyed parties, people, crochet, vegetable gardening, worshipping at Holy Apostles Greek Orthodox church in Westchester, Illinois, and spending time with family.

Grandma Veneta and Alexandra

Nothing Is Impossible with God

It should be noted that in his later writings Luther confirmed a belief in contemporary miracles.[22]

- John Wimber
Power Healing

Judy Schaefer

After suffering for five days with a 99-degree persistent fever and an upset stomach, Judy went to see her primary care physician. He examined her and quickly ascertained that Judy likely had more than just a stubborn flu. He suspected an issue with her internal organs and ordered an immediate abdominal CT scan.

Although Judy was already exhausted, she complied and went to the imaging center that day and had the scan. The technician reported seeing something very concerning, and the doctor asked the technician to also do a pelvic CT scan to be more complete.

The doctors saw a malignant mass on her right kidney and even more serious, a thrombus, i.e., blood clot, in the inferior vena cava. This is a main interior artery to the heart. They thought that cancer had moved into this critical area of her body. The cancer turned out to be renal angiomyolipoma

---

[22] John Wimber and Kevin Springer, *Power Healing*, (New York: HarperCollins, 1987), 11.

and was an extremely aggressive malignancy. It was very bad news.

Judy was so tired and worn out from both the illness as well as the full day of tests that she asked the doctor to give the news to her husband, Jon. Alarmed and vigilant, Jon jumped on the phone and worked to get Judy scheduled as soon as possible to have the cancer surgically removed at one of the two main Chicago area hospitals that could do this specialized surgery. Unfortunately, the earliest he could get surgery scheduled was a month away. Judy was so weak at this point she could barely walk and needed a wheelchair. It was unlikely she would even live another month, let alone survive an intense surgery in her weakened state.

Jon and Judy asked their faith community to pray. And people prayed—a lot of people. One of Judy's favorite verses, which encouraged her was, "Fear not, I am the one who helps you" (Isaiah 41:13, ESV). She also often pondered, "Nothing is impossible with God" (Luke 1:37, NASB).

Then, out of the blue, a urologist they had never met or heard of called and reported that he was able to arrange for not just one doctor, but a team of doctors to remove the kidney, cancer, and do the necessary open-heart surgery in only eleven days at the University of Chicago. Jon and Judy were elated. This was an unexpected and miraculous answer to their prayers. The urologist had been contacted by Judy's primary care physician, and even though he didn't know Judy or even saw her, he made all of this happen for her.

The next fear was whether Judy would live through the surgery, since Judy was so weak and some people who have this surgery do not live through the process. Not only did Judy survive, but it took only six hours instead of the expected nine hours. During the surgery, the doctors found that the cancer had metastasized to two chambers of her heart, but miraculously, when they removed the kidney, the tumor just slid on out with it, even removing from the inferior vena cava and from the heart. It was uncanny and amazing.

Judy made a surprisingly quick recovery, going home after only six days in the hospital.

However, four months later when Judy went in for one of her follow-up scans, the doctors saw again a scary thrombus in the inferior vena cava. Judy's oncologist then prescribed a medication regiment with Everolimus to reduce the spread of cancer in case any remained in her body along with blood thinners.

Every scan since that time in 2017 has shown no change in the images. The doctors have now concluded that what they had been seeing was in fact just scar tissue.

Judy is still cancer-free today. While she always has had a strong faith in God, experiencing His amazing live-saving provision at exactly when she needed it has added another level of assuredness to her faith. Her connection with God's love is even stronger and deeper.

I once heard a friend say sometimes we need to be the miracle. God can use us to bring a miracle to another person, as did the urologist who decided to go above and beyond for a lady who wasn't his patient and he had never even met.

Perhaps we can be providers of miracles for others if we listen to the prodding of God on our hearts and act.

Sometimes we need to be the miracle.

In those days Hezekiah became sick and was at the point of death. Then Hezekiah turned his face to the wall and prayed to the Lord. And Hezekiah wept bitterly. Then the word of the Lord came to Isaiah: "Go and say to Hezekiah, thus says the Lord, the God of David your father: I have heard your prayer; I have seen your tears. Behold, I will add fifteen years to your life."
—Isaiah 38:1-2, 4-5, ESV

Love Miracles

> If you don't think you can have something good, then you never will. The barrier is in your mind.[23]
>
> - Joel Osteen
> *Your Best Life Now*

Alexandra Georgas

As I approached my late thirties, I started to ponder why I hadn't found a long-term love. I examined my dating history and observed that I kept dating guys that I knew I could eventually reject and break up with. They all had obvious features that were not a match for me. Why did I keep picking these guys? I realized it was my fear of intimacy. After experiencing my childhood family blown apart by divorce, I was carrying my crippling fear of letting myself trust and love. Once I figured that out, I said to God, "Okay, Lord. I am the one not letting love in. I keep running from the guys who would be good for me and only dating the ones who I know aren't a match. The next nice guy you bring to me, no matter how scared I am, I will force myself to date him and give it a chance."

I figured God would take His time about it but to my surprise, a week later I met a very nice guy. We talked for four hours during our first dinner together. His loving heart

---

[23] Joel Osteen, *Your Best Life Now*, (New York, FaithWords, 2004), 3.

welcomed me to give love a serious try. We became best friends and married the next year. I learned from this experience that God is ready to give us love. We may be the ones throwing up the walls, as I was.

I was deeply grateful for my sweet, loving man. Marriage was more than I dreamed it could be. But after six happy years, we entered a difficult era. Don was diagnosed with colorectal cancer. We began a new journey of loads and loads of chemo treatments after six weeks of radiation and a major surgery. After fighting for quite a while, during a Good Friday service at our church, our minister broke away from the normal liturgy and spontaneously prayed for healing of people in the congregation. I gently laid my hand on Don as he prayed, as did the kind ladies standing behind us. We prayed that healing would flow through to Don.

Don's doctor had regular tests to see what was happening with his cancer. Up until that prayer, they all showed the cancer was still active. But after that service, the next test showed no cancer, and the next, and the next. We were elated. Don's oncologist was surprised and shared with us that this remission was very unusual. We thanked God for His mercy on us, giving us a much-needed rest from the battle.

That remission lasted an unusually long year and a half, but then the cancer came back. At that point, the doctor gave my husband only three years to live. I then sunk into a depression like I had never experienced before. The pain was so strong that sometimes I thought about ending my life, just to stop the pain. I never would actually do that, I just felt like doing it. The sadness felt like a constant, heavy weight.

I then realized I needed to do something to help myself get through it all. I joined a support group for people who had a loved one with cancer, which was a tremendous help. Don and I also went to a therapist who turned out to be a huge help to us both. The therapist encouraged us to live life to the fullest no matter what happened. We went on six cruises during those cancer years, traveling in the periodic breaks between the many rounds of chemo treatments. We threw lots of parties and celebrated every day. And, my doctor gave me a mild anti-anxiety/anti-depression medication, which helped the most. The medicine really helped pull me out of that pit of pain. The sadness left, and I felt more energy to help Don fight.

Our love bond was strong, but one of the consequences to the surgery and radiation was that Don lost the ability to have sexual intimacy. It was a great loss for us both. But I used to tell him I was thankful for the surgical changes to his body because it meant I still had him.

However, I found myself struggling with the loss of sexual intimacy and the wonderful physical closeness we used to have. Don was so drained and tired from the chemo. He often couldn't do much more than sleep. I was focused on keeping him alive and neglected my own needs quite a bit. We were both often depleted.

Then, one day at work a sexy divorced guy came over to my desk and gave me a look up and down like one does when they really like what they see. I found myself uncomfortably liking that attention. It felt so flattering to know that someone found me that attractive; although, I felt guilty for liking it. He continued to give me flirty attention, and I found myself soaking it up like a dry sponge. I felt terrible enjoying his playfulness knowing my beloved husband was just trying to survive. I felt very conflicted. It felt like another stressful burden I had to battle on top of working hard to help my husband battle cancer.

This inappropriate office flirting went on for months. I found myself having a crush on the office man and wishing so much I didn't. I just couldn't shake it. And he just wouldn't leave me alone, even though I was married and tending to my man who was fighting terminal cancer.

One day, I decided I had had enough. I decided to fast and pray for God to help me. I chose to just fast during the morning, and end the fast at lunch on that day, because we had a team lunch planned.

At the team lunch at the end of my fast, the man confessed to me that he had a girlfriend. I felt a massive smile stretch wider than my whole head. What a great relief! He had someone else special to him. I was elated. And the news instantly killed the crush. I was free. And my freedom came at the exact end of my fast. God moved the man to admit he was in fact just screwing with me. I practically skipped back to the office that day in celebration. The crush was crushed, and after that, he finally stopped leading me on.

I'm so glad that I never did have even a lunch date with the guy, let alone have any date with him or cheat with him. God protected me and my marriage, which I was deeply grateful for. And I was so grateful he finally left me alone! As a matter of fact, I am thankful God has helped me to have never cheated on anyone I was dating, let alone married to.

Don and I fought with all we had, turning to clinical trials when the standard treatments were no longer effective. We had two mottos: "No stone unturned" and "Let's go down swinging." We looked into all suggested helps and fought hard. My sweet Don did finally pass away from cancer six years after the doctor gave him only three years to live. I entered a different kind of sadness at that point. It was not overwhelming, just there, flowing in and out with gentle tides of tears. I joined another support group, this time for people who lost a spouse to cancer. It was a great safe place to let out the tears. I felt comforted and consoled.

Since I knew for so long that Don would die from cancer, I grieved a lot while he was still around, while battling depression. I noticed that I seemed to be further along in my mourning process than other people in my support group who had lost their spouses in a much shorter amount of time. I found that after a couple of years, I was ready to love again. But I knew that finding a life partner was no easy task, and I really wanted God to guide me in my search. As usual, I prayed.

A guy at work organized a weekly prayer group, which I joined. I was the only woman in the group of all married, computer technology men. Every week I asked them to pray for God to lead me to a good man to love. And these faith-filled, work brothers of mine did pray for many months.

Right before Christmas, my stepdaughter and her husband were both laid off from the same restaurant where they both worked. When I went to visit at New Years, I took them to a grocery store and bought them a boat load of groceries, treated them to dinners out, and helped them out as much as I could. After the holidays, I mailed them a check for $500 to help them in their transition time. My stepdaughter at first showed great appreciation, lovingly thanking me for my help. But then a few weeks later, she shocked me with a three-page letter accusing me of seventeen outlandish acts. The surprising letter was both disturbing and cruel. She made it very clear in her letter that I was no longer wanted in her life.

I immediately reached out to try to work this out with her but was swiftly rejected with more harsh cruelty. She was not open to any sort of peaceful resolution.

The worse part about it was that not only did I lose her, but I lost my two grandchildren from this surprising act. She had two beautiful kids whom I absolutely adored and poured all my grandmotherly love onto. In one act, they were all cut out from my life.

It took me a few years to no longer feel angry and hurt over this painful act. But at this point, now many years later, I see my stepdaughter as a young woman who is suffering herself, with a lot of unresolved stuff that fed into her committing this act. And she lost having another person in her life who had her back and loved her. I feel sorry for her that she harmed herself, her kids, as well as me in her actions. She made her love circle smaller for her family.

But I also know that God allows things for a purpose. I can see now that she was not a safe person for me, and God protected me by allowing her to do this terrible thing to me. God allowed her to do this to me so I would not waste my love on someone who was really just using me and not able to love me in return. I have chosen to forgive her and let it go. But even so, after losing my husband, it was quite major to lose those two little ones as well.

About a month after this rejection, Lent began. During that six-week holy time, I fasted for two meals on one day of each week and spent greater time on those days asking God to lead me to a person to love and marry. On the last week of Lent, while hanging out with my dad, who was weak from fighting advanced prostate cancer, I decided to have Dad help me look at the guys online. "This one is a biker, Dad. What do you think?"

Dad laughed and answered, "I don't know, not sure that one's for you."

Then I found a guy who wrote some things I liked about being a father, person of faith, and that he had a lot of hobbies. I liked the idea of guy who had his own interests like that. "Check out this guy Dad, what do you think?" I asked.

Dad weakly replied, "He's nice, whatever makes you happy."

I went ahead and gave the man a virtual "wink" through the web site.

The next day, which was the exact last day of my Lent fasting, Roger responded. Just the day before, he had given up on the idea of finding a woman, and had prayed, "God, I give up. If you want me to marry again, you'll need to bring a woman to me."

On the day my fast ended, Roger started deleting all of his dating site stuff but then saw my virtual "wink." He almost hit "delete" but then was drawn to my screen name of "Happy Girl." Being the sarcastic, wise-ass man that he is, he couldn't resist teasing me about my made-up screen name. We playfully texted over the site, progressed to talking on the phone, and met a few days later. I was hesitant at first, but after the encouragement of a friend, I decided to give it a go.

On another day during our dating time, I gave up two meals to fast again and asked God to guide me as to whether I should marry Roger. On that very day, Roger told me with great conviction that he was sure that he wanted to marry me. I believed God encouraged me to keep moving forward towards that end.

On June 6 the next year, we married in the same church where my parents and grandparents married and we are still happily married today. God most definitely heard our prayers and gave us to each other. And He did so on the exact last day of my Lenten fast for a husband and encouraged me on the very day I later fasted and prayed, asking for direction. And He did so right after I suffered the major blow of being attacked and cut off from people I loved dearly.

My oldest grandchild left his parent's home a few years ago. Instantly, I started searching to see if just maybe I could be a part of his life now that he was out of his parent's house. Although I did have some idea of where he was, he chose to live a bit off the grid for a while making it impossible to find him. I kept searching and not only did I find him, I contacted him and to my absolute delight, he was happy I did. The first day we talked nearly two hours on the phone getting caught up from our seven years apart. I am deeply grateful to have him back in my life again. Some years were lost, and some things have changed, but our love for one another never ceased, and we enjoy each other so much now.

There is a verse in the Bible that I think of a lot when I reflect on this part of my life. "I will repay you for the years the locusts have eaten" (Joel 2:25, NIV). This verse refers to a locust's plague that had destroyed the crops and people had no food, but God promised to make up for the devastation. God certainly did that in my life by giving me my new sweet husband, who brought with him his three great sons, our daughter-in-law, a new grandson, and our twin grandbabies. And on top of all that, I now have my older grandson back in my life. God has restored what was taken away and provided even more. God led and we are all so blessed as a result.

Alexandra and Roger

Too Good To Be True

Things are possible for the person who has hope. Even more is possible for the person who has faith. Still more is possible for the person who knows how to love.[24]

- Brother Lawrence
  The Practice of the Presence of GOD

Alexandra Georgas and Mark Bankhead

Roger and I needed a third player for our Tuesday night bowling league. The league leaders let us know they found someone to complete our team a few weeks after the league had started. We were so happy to have a full team.

Kathy had just moved to the Chicago area from Houston. She was getting out of her home a lot to enjoy life and meet new people, including in our bowling league. Kathy was a beautiful African-American woman with a quiet disposition. I was happy to have a new girlfriend to get to know as we played. I found out that she was in her younger fifties, lived with her aging parents, was a church going person of faith, had an adult son who she was quite close with, and was a widow. She worked in the healthcare field as a caregiver in an assisted living facility. Her late husband had been a medical research doctor. I had lost my first husband ten years earlier

---

[24] Brother Lawrence, T*he Practice of the Presence OF GOD*, (New Kensington, PA, Whitaker House, 1982), 25.

and knew firsthand how painful it was to lose the man I loved, plus at a relatively young age. It's not fun.

Meanwhile, Roger's best buddy, Mark, had recently lost his wife to cancer. Roger and I had tried to get him to bowl with us, but he wasn't ready to re-enter bowling after the years he spent caring for his ill wife. Mark was a handsome African-American man in his fifties.

Once I learned Kathy was a widow, I thought of Mark. I told Kathy about him. "Roger's best friend lost his wife recently to cancer, and he's about your age. He's a really good guy. But I'm not sure if he's ready to date just yet. It's only been a few months."

I didn't mention his race.

Kathy thought, *He must be a white guy if she called him "a good guy."* She dismissed it as an unlikely connection.

I suggested to Roger, "I wonder if Kathy and Mark might like each other. They seem to have some similarities, like they are both people of faith, both widows, around the same age, and have adult children."

Roger then told Mark, "You should come visit us at bowling. Our teammate, Kathy, is a young widow and she's sweet. You should come meet her."

Mark was surprised at the notion, and pondered, *Am I ready for that?* But then he thought, *It'll be a new year soon. Maybe it's time for new things in my life.* He waited to visit the week of Roger's birthday, December 22. He didn't want to appear too eager, so he thought that would look like a good excuse for a visit.

Once he saw Kathy, he thought, *Oh no. She is way out of my league. She must have someone in her life. She is gorgeous.*

He sat with Roger and talked with him the whole night.

I told Kathy, "That's the guy I was telling you about. Mark is Roger's best friend. He's really a great guy."

Kathy thought, *What? He's Black? She didn't tell me that. Wow. I need to let him know I am interested!*

Kathy was pretty shy, but she forced herself to flirt with him and try to let him know she was interested.

After bowling was over, Mark had to go another way because he parked in a different parking lot than the rest of us. Kathy and Mark were both disappointed they had to part.

About a week later, Roger and I both came down with a mild case of COVID-19. We skipped bowling that week, of course. Mark texted Roger to see how he was doing, and at the exact same time, Kathy was texting me.

Kathy asked: *Is Mark coming next Tuesday as far as you know?*

I replied, *He said he's not coming this Tuesday. I'm almost back to normal now too. Just a tiny sniffle and I had full energy today.*

Kathy wrote: *Okay. I'm glad you are feeling better. I was hoping I got a chance to see him. But okay.*

He'll be back, I assured.

Okay, tell him to call me, Kathy said.

We're texting him now, I said.

Roger texted Kathy's phone number to Mark and wrote, *She says she wants you to call her.*

Mark then called Roger to confirm what he read and to talk about that idea.

Then I texted Kathy: *Roger is on the phone with Mark. We gave him your number. He said he can't call today. He's been sick too so he's getting over that, and I think he's going somewhere today. Now he said he may come on Tuesday, too. How fun!!*

After that texting and talking exchange, Mark did call Kathy. They connected instantly. And they have talked every single day since, and that was on January 7, 2023.

They bonded over sharing what it was like to love a spouse and then lose them due to illness, although Mark's wife was sick for many years and Kathy's husband's passing was from a complete surprise of heart failure. They also found ways they are great for one another that are rather surprising. Mark is a repairman who has to drive to many places every day for his job. On the weekends, he doesn't like to drive anywhere. To his great delight, Kathy loves to drive and prefers to drive them. They were also happily surprised to find out they both love to relax listening to jazz music.

Their families are happy and supportive of them, including Mark's late wife's family who welcomed Kathy and expressed great happiness for them both. Roger and I are both thrilled to see them both find love again. Mark calls us his Cupids.

I asked Mark if he had any miracle stories for my book and he answered, "Yes, me and Kathy. There are so many ways we are right for each other. This had to be God. The way Roger was texting me at the exact time you were texting Kathy, how unlikely was that? This was God all the way."

I do believe that God loves to give people one another to love. He is the ultimate and best matchmaker. And when He gives a gift, He gives a good gift. It warms my heart to know we helped those two find one another and have a deep and growing love for each other. And for that, we all are truly grateful.

"Every good thing given and every perfect gift is from above, coming down from the Father of lights, with whom there is no variation or shifting shadow."
—James 1:17, NASB

Mark Bankhead has worked as a service technician for thirty-five years. He has one daughter, a stepson, and three grandchildren. He enjoys bowling, jazz music, and spending time with friends and family.

Prayers in the Night

> It's not only that we need to return to a mutual respect between science and religion, but the healing of suffering people requires both—medical treatment as well as prayer. [25]
>
> - Francis MacNutt
>   *Healing*

Anonymous

Rebecca and Sarah were traveling together, with their young children in the back seat of the car. Nearby a man was speeding in his vehicle at a very high rate and driving erratically because he was being chased by a police cruiser. The man's car crashed at full speed into the passenger side of Sarah's car, right where Rebecca was sitting. Sarah suffered a broken hip, but Rebecca had extensive injuries including severe brain trauma. Fortunately, the children all had no injuries.

Rebecca was in a coma in the intensive care unit of the hospital, and the doctors did not expect her to live. However, Rebecca had been very involved both in her church and an interdenominational prayer group, which got together often to pray. She was well-loved by all in these communities, and many prayed for her. She also had a praying nurse who was caring for her in the ICU.

---

[25] Francis MacNutt, PhD., *Healing* (Notre Dame, Indiana: Ave Maria Press, 1999), 215.

One night, Rebecca was struggling and was fading. Her nurse could see that it was unlikely she would make it through the night. She whispered prayers for her as she tended to her, asking for God to heal Rebecca. At the exact same time, Rebecca's friend Mary woke in the night and felt moved to pray for Rebecca. Several other praying friends also woke abruptly and felt moved to pray for Rebecca, all at that same time in the night.

Rebecca lived through that night. There were other nights when the praying friends were awakened in the night to pray, which they did. Every time they learned later that at those times was when Rebecca was doing poorly and in greater risk of dying. Yet every time, Rebecca pulled through.

After just three weeks after being in the ICU, Rebecca was moved to the brain injury section of the rehabilitation facility. She recovered fully. The discharge staff shared that they didn't expect anyone else on her floor of severely injured patients to ever be released. She was the only one on the floor who was restored to full functionality.

Rebecca later married and had three more children and continues to show no signs of effects from the severe accident.

"[P]ray for each other so that you may be healed. The earnest prayer of a righteous person has great power and produces wonderful results."
—James 5:16, NLT

Baby Protection

> It is fascinating that when I ask an audience how many of them believe that they have had a direct encounter with an evil spirit, about one third of them usually raise their hands.[26]
>
> - Francis MacNutt
>   *Healing*

Pastor Paul Horstmeyer

In 2017, one of Pastor Paul's fellow seminarian couples had their first baby during their second year in seminary. Things were smooth for the three of them in their first weeks together. They had baby Alexander baptized when he was about a month-and-a-half old. The night after his baptism, however, he had what seemed to be night terrors. He was inconsolable. His mom Ashley did all the normal things—feed, change, rock, swaddle, etc.—but nothing calmed down little baby Alexander. This was quite out of character for him. Then she had a sense that there was something spiritual going on. She began to pray over Alexander and even called on Jesus's name for protection against evil spiritual forces. As soon as she prayed, he calmed. This continued for a few more nights, where Alexander would be in terror, and his mother would pray over him, and he was better. Finally, the terrors ceased for good. Ashley's conclusion was it seemed to be spiritual

---

[26] Francis MacNutt, PhD., *Healing* (Notre Dame, Indiana: Ave Maria Press, 1999), 174.

forces attacking a new child of God. It's hard to know for sure, but nothing but Mom's prayers solved the dilemma.

Alexander has had no night terrors since that time, and he loves to attend church with his parents. They are all happily following the Lord.

Jesus said, "Let the little children come to me, and do not hinder them, for the kingdom of heaven belongs to such as these."
—Matthew 19:14, NIV

Paul Horstmeyer is a pastor at Trinity Lutheran Church in Lisle, Illinois. He and his wife Mary have three children and enjoy spending time with family and friends.

We pray for little children,
too young
to pray for themselves.[27]
written by young people in Kenya

---

[27] Angela Ashwin, *The Book of a Thousand Prayers*, (Grand Rapids, Michigan, Zondervan, 2002), 189.

Joyful Perseverance

> The difficulties of life do not have to be unbearable. It is the way we look at them—through faith or unbelief—that makes them seem so.[28]
>
> - Brother Lawrence
>   *The Practice of the Presence of GOD*

Anonymous

Around 2002, George's pastor asked if he and his wife, Jan, could help out Laurel, a woman in need of a helping hand. Laurel's husband had been killed in a car accident, and she had also lost her daughter at the young age of seventeen from a brain hemorrhage. To make matters even worse, she lost her son to suicide, and she was on disability due to having Guillain-Barre syndrome. In about 2000, her illness had progressed, and her finances decreased such that she was no longer able to live alone in her house.

Fortunately, she received the blessing of being able to move into a federally funded housing unit where rent was based on a percentage of her income. Laurel was extremely thankful for her new home. Even with all of these losses and challenges in her life, Laurel was always cheerful and upbeat. She was a surprisingly happy person. Then in 2018, Laurel was diagnosed with Multiple Myeloma cancer. She was in and out

---

[28] Brother Lawrence, *The Practice of the Presence OF GOD*, (New Kensington, PA, Whitaker House, 1982), 55.

of the hospital, and the vertebrae in her back began to crumble. Even still, Laurel shined with an inspirational, cheerful, and upbeat attitude. Her smiles lifted the spirits of all she met. She never complained once. And through it all, her church community prayed often for Laurel.

Laurel decided to not attempt surgery but rather opt for rehabilitation with a back brace. She was admitted to St. Patrick's Catholic rehabilitation center in Naperville, Illinois, a highly rated facility. But Laurel was not there long and tried to return to her apartment. A few days later, a health department worker checked up on her and saw that Laurel was not doing well. They contacted George, who took Laurel to the nearby hospital emergency room where she was admitted.

The doctors decided to try to attempt surgery to help strengthen her back, fondly referred to as a "cement job". However, as soon as they cut open her body, she bled uncontrollably. They had to abruptly halt the surgery.

Laurel accepted from this experience that she could no longer live independently in her apartment. However, since she was living on Medicaid, her options were limited. George helped her apply to several nursing home facilities in the area to see if they had any Medicaid beds available. Laurel was moved back to St. Patrick's for more rehab. George didn't consider St. Pat's a long-term option for Laurel since St. Pat's was a five-star rated facility and Laurel had no private funds or insurance. One day, the administrator asked, "Why don't you submit a Medicaid application here?"

George applied for Laurel but didn't think that was possible. As the search continued, time was running out. Her stay at St. Pat's was almost over.

Suddenly, with a few days left on her rehabilitation stay, the nurse at St. Pat's shared with George matter-of-factly, "Oh, we moved Laurel upstairs."

They never actually said her application had been accepted. Something moved them to provide a private room for her, and it was adjacent to the nurse's station, a great place to be for the best attentive care.

Laurel was ecstatic. She loved the center, already knew the staff, and felt very at home at the warm place. The facility was very clean, had great food, and lots of social activities. Laurel spent the last five months of her earthly life there. She was greatly cared for in that special community.

I suppose some could argue there are no miracles in this story. A woman suffered all her life and passed away. But I see several signs of the miraculous and supernatural. I see a perfect home opening up for a woman who had a life of suffering and limited resources just when she needed it. She had a place of peace for her end of days. God provided that for her, as many in her church community were praying for her to have just that. That was a beautiful answer to prayer. And I see Laurel's cheerfulness, even though her life circumstances were full of loss and difficulty, as another miracle. She grew in her faith in God through her life challenges and leaned on God, and God gave her joy even when she had great hardship. Perhaps that is the greatest miracle.

"In all this you greatly rejoice, though now for a little while you may have had to suffer grief in all kinds of trials. These have come so that the proven genuineness of your faith—of greater worth than gold, which perishes even though refined by fire—may result in praise, glory and honor when Jesus Christ is revealed."
—I Peter 1:6-7, NIV

Part IV

Divine Direction, God's Humor, Overcoming Evil and Lack of Faith

Not a Secret to God

Alexandra Georgas

I was overweight during my high school years and like many teens, very insecure about myself. My energies went into the challenges I was facing having a mom who was disabled with a severe mental illness. I didn't have any courage to pursue any boys, and not many were looking my way.

When I was nineteen and in college, I joined Weight Watchers for the first time. I lost seventy pounds and went from a chubby nerd to an attractive, skinny nerd. Boys and men started to notice me a lot more, and I found myself getting asked out on dates. I enjoyed all the new attention.

I worked as a crew chief at McDonald's part time to help pay for books, gas, and other college expenses. One of my bosses asked me to go to a festival with him. Since he was engaged and living with his girlfriend, I figured he just wanted to be friends with me. That is, I thought that until on the date when he parked in a secluded spot and kissed me. My naïve teenage mind was quite surprised.

I didn't necessarily find him all that attractive. He was just kind of okay looking and a bit closed-off. But I liked being kissed for a change. I had missed out on all the dating that I watched my friends engage in when in high school. I was curious about sex, having only been kissed by three guys prior. I decided I wanted to find out what all this dating stuff was. But I also knew that since he was engaged, this was wrong. We were betraying someone. Even so, I agreed to keep seeing him.

I asked him that we keep it a secret, and he heartily agreed. But we were hurting ourselves and his fiancée. Not one of my better life choices.

I saw him about once a week where he basically would take me somewhere and we'd just make out. A couple times we'd just go driving around on his motorcycle then park somewhere to neck. Another time on his jeep. Every time we'd advance further and further, but never more than kissing and petting.

Then he somehow got a van, and we drove off and parked. We went further that day than any of the previous times, although still not to the point of orgasms or intercourse. Just a lot of necking and petting.

When I arrived back home after that van encounter, I found myself having a strange feeling that came over me. It was a very strong, inner heaviness. I didn't feel guilt, sad, or anything physical. It was just an inner burden that I have never experienced any other time in my life.

I questioned out loud, "Lord, what is this?"

I then flipped open my Bible, and my eyes fell right on these verses:

"But each one is tempted when he is carried away and enticed by his own lust. Then when lust has conceived it gives birth to sin, and when sin is accomplished, it brings forth death. Do not be deceived, my beloved brethren." —James 1:14-16 NASB

Holy moly was that ever a conviction. I mean God himself directed me to this perfect verse to open up my eyes to where I was heading. I was being enticed by my own lust. If I continued seeing him, I would eventually sin—have sex without love and life commitment. That would hurt me to the point it would harm me spiritually—my relationship with God would suffer and die. I was being deceived. But he still called me His beloved. God didn't hate me. God loved me. I'm His "beloved." It was a loving, kind rebuke.

I told God, "Got it, Lord. I will not see him again."

I figured God would punish me by being sure I didn't date for a long time. But no, God is not like that. God is loving and wants us to have love. Within a week, I met a new guy who I actually fell in love with. He was my first real love.

When the engaged guy asked me out again, I told him I would not see him anymore. He asked, "It is because you have a boyfriend now?" and I replied, "No, it's because it's wrong."

He just shrugged as if my words were meaningless to him. I noticed him flirting with another female crew member within a few days. He just moved onto a new conquest.

I happened to see him years after that. He did marry his fiancée. They had been youth leaders in their church. But he also had a P.O. box for his address. In hindsight, I wish I had spoken up to have him investigated. My silence was a poor choice.

My new boyfriend was trying to not be gay. He was dating me but attracted to guys. I absolutely loved who he was. He was a funny, playful, energetic, and sweet-hearted guy. But when he kissed me, it was like kissing a board. Not very satisfying. Yet, because we loved each other, I was satisfied just being with him. I learned how sexual contact without love is empty but love without sexual contact can be so fulfilling. It is a million times better.

We dated for a summer, and I broke it off when I went away to an out-of-the area university. I saw him about six years later, and he was only dating guys at that point. I knew I made the best decision to break up with him years earlier. I wished him well. When I think of him now, I have warm, happy memories of him. He will always hold a special place in my heart.

I dated many more guys after that. I had a desire to stay a virgin until I was married for a number of reasons. One is that I chose to respect my body enough to not let it be used as a sex object. I understood a beautiful bond that can develop between two people who love one another, are strongly committed to each other, and then make love. The emotional satisfaction is like nothing else. That's what I wanted. But I didn't marry until I was thirty-eight years old. I dated lots of temping, beautiful men over the years. I did have a lot of fun with the guys I was serious about, but amazingly I was able to keep intercourse off the table until my wedding day. I gotta say, I think that was another miracle, especially in this day and age. But I'm so glad I waited. Intimacy with my husband was so special and meaningful to us both. It was a great gift I gave to myself as well as to him. I don't think I could have done that without God's help, not only with dating the engaged guy, but over all those single years. And for that I am forever grateful.

"For the kingdom of God is not a matter of talk but of power."
—I Corinthians 4:20, NIV

Healing Wounded Hearts

> Instead of being forced to the extremes of Western empiricism or Eastern animism, the Bible allows for the possibility, though not the necessity, of supernatural intervention in all earthly experience.[29]
>
> - John Wimber
>   *Power Evangelism*

Judy

Judy and her three siblings grew up in poverty in the southwestern suburb of Chicago then called Stickney, now named Burbank. They had no running water in the house, had to use an outhouse in the backyard, and had tar paper floors. Even one neighbor was so disgusted with their home she created a petition to have them removed and went around the neighborhood trying to get everyone to sign it, which was not successful.

Judy's father had abandoned the family and provided no support of any kind. Her mother worked in a factory and was not able to tend much to her children, leaving for work before they came home from school, and she would return from work after they were asleep. They were on their own, kids raising kids. The children had each other, but they fought

---

[29] John Wimber and John Springer, *Power Evangelism* (Minneapolis, Chosen Books, 2009), 138.

a lot, with no one there to referee. Judy felt very unloved and rejected especially by her father.

Judy found out years later that her father lived only a few miles away with another woman with which he had six more children. He never even visited Judy and her siblings.

One day Judy needed a ride so badly she resorted to calling her father for help. He came and drove her but scolded her the whole way about how she would now make him late to work. More rejection.

When Judy was fourteen years old, her mother had arranged for her to do housework for her uncle while he was at work. While working in his home a heavy fear came over her, and she had to leave immediately. She was greatly fearful that he would come home. What was she so afraid of?

As an adult, she had a dream that this same uncle was trying to get her. She was hiding under her bed. All he was wearing was his underwear. She wondered if the dream was hinting that he had abused her. Even though the dream was disturbing in nature, Judy experienced God's light protecting her, and she felt no fear in the dream.

She later went to a seminar on sexual abuse and found herself crying as if it had happened to her. She wondered if she had been abused, and her mind wouldn't let her remember. Then her cousin confessed to her that the uncle had sexually abused her. Judy knew then that it did in fact happen to her and found herself crying continuously for the next two weeks. This was another major hurt that added to the emotional pain Judy carried.

On occasion, Judy's grandmother and step-grandmother took her and her siblings to their respective Pentecostal churches, and there were occasions when each of the two grandmothers spoke in tongues over Judy. Judy found the behavior to be terrifying. While Judy believed in God, she was afraid to follow Christianity because she didn't want to be anything like her radical grandmothers.

Judy graduated high school and found a job at a gas company in the accounting department. It was the only job Judy would ever have for her entire life. One of the handsome men at work was smitten by Judy. They started dating, fell deeply in love, and married in 1973.

Judy still felt the void in her heart from her parentless childhood, sexual abuse, and lack of true connection with God. She started seeking God, first by reading the Bible and then by attending a Bible church with her husband. She then went to a women's retreat and heard a woman named Kay Arthur speak about being a "living sacrifice." Kay Arthur has written many excellent Bible study guides. Judy pondered what that might mean. After the talk, Judy sought out Kay who spent time sharing with Judy what it means to truly be a Christian and follow God in your life. That night, Judy knelt at home and told God, "Okay, Lord, yes. I want my life to be a living sacrifice to you."

Judy would never be the same.

Meanwhile Judy's husband was opening his heart up to faith as well. After the church showed a convictional movie one Sunday, he made a renewed commitment to follow God.

The young couple wanted to have a family, but after quite some time, they realized it was not meant to be. They just couldn't get pregnant.

Then in Judy's daily Bible reading, she found Isaiah 58:7-8, ESV.

> *Is it not to share your bread with the hungry,*
> *and <u>bring the homeless poor into your house</u>;*
> *when you see the naked, to cover him,*
> *and not to hide yourself from your own flesh?*
> *Then shall your light break forth like the dawn,*
> *<u>and your healing shall spring up speedily</u>;*
> *your righteousness shall go before you,*
> *the glory of the* Lord *shall be your rear guard.*

She knew that she needed inner healing. She pondered, *This verse says that to bring the homeless poor into my home will bring healing in my life. How do we do this? What does this mean for us?*

Judy's husband had four children from his previous marriage, and one was not doing very well. They wondered if this verse meant that they should pursue custody of that child. They also wondered if they should become foster parents. They pursued both. They made an appointment with ECFA, the Evangelical Child and Family Association, who had picked two foster kids to live with them. They wondered, though, if it would make sense to take in foster children when one of the children needed his dad so much at that time. At the appointment, the ECFA counsellor advised that they should not become foster parents but rather spend their energy helping the son. They did just that. Unfortunately, the son's mother would not agree to let the son live with them, but they were still able to provide their love and attention to him.

Time passed, the son left his mother's home and went out on his own. Judy then went to another women's retreat in Chattanooga, at Kay Arthur's complex. Hundreds of women attended the conference. As Judy sat in the large auditorium, she noticed every woman there was white, except one lady. One Black lady sat by herself way across the auditorium. Judy looked at her and became overcome with sadness and felt a strong desire to cry. "Why am I feeling so sad as I look at that lady, God?" she questioned. It made no sense to her.

"Lord, if you want me to meet her, you work it out. Bring her to me." Judy prayed.

The weekend retreat continued. During a Saturday morning session, the lady came up and sat right next to Judy. Of all the people the lady could have chosen, why her? The leader asked the ladies, "If you do not know the person sitting next to you, introduce yourself."

Judy turned to the lady and greeted her saying, "I'm Judy. What's your name?"

The lady was so shy she could not even speak or look at Judy. But she wrote out her name on a piece of paper and gave it to Judy.

Luella, from Nashville, she had written.

"Nice to meet you Luella," Judy welcomed.

Luella continued to stare at the ground.

Judy didn't see Luella after they broke for lunch nor in the next session. Around 3:00 p.m., there was a break from the teaching sessions. Judy went out with her friends to the courtyard, and she spotted Luella not far away. Judy thought, *Maybe I should ask her for her address.*

Luella was talking with some other ladies, and Judy didn't want to interfere with their connecting time. Judy prayed, "Lord, if it is your will for me to ask her for her address would you make that happen?"

When you feel compassion toward someone, that's God's way of telling you to be a blessing to that person. Go encourage them. See how you can make his or her life better.[30]

More time passed, and Judy didn't see Luella anywhere. On the last day, Sunday, the conference was over and almost everyone had left. Judy was about to leave the empty auditorium when in came Luella waving a piece of paper in the air and declaring, "Judy, Judy, I want your address!"

As Judy was writing down her address she wondered, *Do I really want to give her my phone number too? That might not be wise.*

---

[30] Joel Osteen, *Your Best Life Now,* (New York, FaithWords, 2004), 244.

Then the Lord said to Judy, *Judy, you promised me you'd do anything I'd ask you to do.* Judy said in her heart, *Yes Lord*, and wrote down both her address and her phone number.

Judy was still on the road back to Chicago when she checked in on the phone with her husband to let him know they were safely on their way. He reported, "Some woman from the retreat called for you."

Judy replied, "I know who that is. I'll tell you about it when I get home."

Judy told her travel friends about the whole experience and jokingly added, "She probably wants to live with us."

As she articulated that the Lord spoke to her, *This is the one.* Judy knew this was the person that the Lord wanted her to bring into her home to care for. She didn't tell her husband. Like Mary, the mother of Jesus, when she was told she was to bear the Christ child, she told no one but pondered it all in her heart. Judy kept all it inside.

Two weeks later Luella came to visit. Judy learned that Luella was twenty-eight years old. Her life had been full of many dark things, which little by little she confided in Judy.

After seven months of more visits and daily phone calls, Luella called Judy one day and declared, "Judy, I can't take it anymore. I have got to get out of here. Can I please come stay with you?"

Judy replied, "I need you to ask my husband. He is the head of our home, and it's his call."

So, Luella asked him if she could come and stay with them.

Judy's husband wasn't keen on the idea, but he knew how convicted Judy was about Luella. He didn't want to get in the way of God doing something good. He concluded, "I will fast and pray about it for three days and let you know." He did just that. He then told Judy, "I'd rather it would just be you and me alone together, but I believe God wants her to come. She can stay for three months, and then she'll need to find a place of her own."

Luella came the day after her birthday. Everyone was nervous, and especially anxious Luella, who didn't trust anyone. She also related to the couple as her family of origin did with her, with critical meanness. She was not easy to live with. She was very fearful and vented that fear by kicking things, complaining, attacking people verbally. People were afraid of Luella. But Judy kept returning her cutting words with love. As Judy loved Luella, whose childhood was in ways similar to Judy's, they both healed.

Luella grew in confidence, became much kinder, and was very successful working in libraries using her English degree. She became free to live her life as she wanted to, a freedom she had never had with her family of origin or out on her own. She gave back to others, even leading a Bible study herself. Judy had the family she longed for and found it to be deeply fulfilling to care for her new surrogate daughter. As Luella softened, she expressed deep love back to Judy. Their bond healed both of them.

Judy's brother-in-law would have nothing to do with Luella when she first came, and Luella wanted nothing to do with him either. But as Luella received nurturing love from Judy, she grew to the point where she bought the brother-in-law presents and won him over. He's very cool with her now.

Judy is now in her eighties and Luella has retired. They all still live together, over thirty years after that three-month trial and they take care of each other and often share "I love yous" with one another. They are family of mutual love. God took their pain and turned it all into a meaningful healing purpose. They are a living testimony of the transforming, healing power of love.

> "He healeth the broken in heart and bindeth up their wounds."
> —Psalm 147:3 KJV

Judy worked for twenty-nine years in an accounting department at a gas company. She has been married to her husband for fifty-one years. She enjoys helping others and worshipping at their church where they have been members for many years.

Paranormal Assault

> Let no one ever come to you without leaving better and happier.[31]
>
> \- Mother Theresa

Alexandra Georgas

One night I stopped to visit my friend Jim at his apartment in Oak Park, Illinois, after my graduate school class at DePaul University in Chicago. Jim had been my coworker for a few years, and we were friends even longer. He was having a rough time due to being recently laid off. He was quite happy that I dropped in even though I didn't forewarn him of my visit. He invited me in and quickly shared with me about his struggles with the job search and frustration with the whole process. I just listened with care and let him talk. After about an hour, I asked him if I could pray for him. Jim eagerly welcomed my prayer. We spent about another twenty minutes praying for his job search and his anxiety about it all. He expressed thanks over and over as I left. It felt great just to be there for my buddy in need.

After I left, I walked on the sidewalk back to my car and someone shoved me hard on the top of my back. The shove was so forceful that I fell over and landed on my hands and knees. I skinned my knee and put a hole in my nylons. I quickly

---

[31] Mother Theresa, Peggy Anderson, *Great Quotes from Great Women*, (Naperville, Illinois: Simple Truths, 2017), 32.

got up and looked to see who pushed me so hard. There was no one there, no one anywhere around, and the buildings were a good 40 feet from the sidewalk. No one could have hit me and run away fast enough that I would not have seen the assailant. It was so weird. Spooky.

The thought that came to me as an explanation was that I was attacked by a demon of some sort. The evil one did not like it that I helped my buddy with his faith. He literally attacked me for it. I was tempted to be afraid but then I remembered the Scripture that says, "Blessed are those who are persecuted because of righteousness" (Matthew 5:10, NIV). This attack was a confirmation that I had done something good for God, or the evil one would not have been so mad at me.

I also remembered the verse, "[T]hou that inhabitest the praises of Israel" (Psalm 22:3, KJV). That verse encouraged me to play praise music on my radio and sing to God the whole way home. I knew that no devil would want to hang out with me if I was singing praises to God. I slept in a great peace that night. And my friend did find a great new job within a couple of weeks after that night.

A Dream Family

May the wonderful energy of God's healing power flow into you, fill you with new life, and give you peace and calm.[32]

Jenny Price

Jenny was away at college in Paris, France. Her menstruation cycle had always been very regular but suddenly Jenny discovered her system became erratic and unpredictable. This irregularity continued after she graduated and returned home to the United States. She visited her doctor to find out what might be the cause of the issue, but the doctor could not find any obvious reason. She hadn't lost any weight nor was she experiencing much stress. Jenny tracked what was happening to see if there was any sort of pattern, but no pattern emerged. Sometimes there were about 30 days between cycles, sometimes 90, sometimes 120, sometimes longer.

Two years later, Jenny married, and after a few years she and her husband Nick desired to start a family. But, due to Jenny's unreliable menstruation system, they weren't sure if that could happen. They asked the Lord, "What's your definition of family for us, God?"

---

[32] Angela Ashwin, *The Book of a Thousand Prayers*, (Grand Rapids, Michigan, Zondervan, 2002), 234.

They opened their hearts to the idea it might mean options such as adoption or fostering. They kept praying and asking God to lead them to what was best for them.

Jenny's doctor tried progesterone as a treatment plan. Jenny finished the course of treatment, but nothing changed. Then one night she had a dream. At the end of the dream Jenny had a strong impression that she was pregnant. It was such a strong impression that when she woke, she not only remembered the dream and the impression, she felt moved to take a pregnancy test. It was positive. She followed up with her doctor who had her tested, and that test also confirmed that Jenny was in fact pregnant. It was July. Jenny hadn't had any period since January.

Jenny gave birth to baby Abigail the following March, naturally and with no complications. Once Jenny completed breastfeeding, her body finally became regular, and she was no longer having irregular menstruation cycles. She later gave birth to her son, Evan, two years later and later had another daughter, Ariel. Abigail is now thirteen years old, Evan is eleven, and little Ariel is eight.

> "God has heard your prayer. Your wife, Elizabeth, will give you a son, and you are to name him John."
> —Luke 1:13, NLT

Jenny Price currently lives this chapter of life as wife to Nick since 2008, mom to three kids of elementary through high school age and enjoys leading small groups and walking alongside others in their faith. When she isn't driving a minivan full of kids, hiking, or sewing, Jenny loves to share a good cup of tea with a friend. Her favorite Bible verse is John 14:27.

Overcoming Fear

Alexandra Georgas

One night I came home from graduate school late, and, in my garden-level apartment, I worked on practicing a talk I was scheduled to give the next day at work. I could see something rapidly flickering outside my window, in the crack in my curtains that were slightly open. I said to myself, "What the heck is that?" and opened the curtains.

Just outside of my living room window was a man naked from the waist down masturbating. I screamed at the top of my lungs and ran to the telephone. I was so frightened I couldn't even remember how to call 911. I called 411 instead and asked for the number for the police. I was shaking and deeply terrified that he would break in. Finally, my mind cleared, and I called 911 and the police came. I also called my dad who lived less than ten minutes away, who came over immediately. The man fled without trying to break into my apartment. But I was deeply traumatized. I never stayed another night in that apartment. I spent a few weeks at my friends home while I found a new place, on a second floor, in another city and moved.

But even at the new apartment I was afraid to enter alone. I was so deeply violated by this horrible man. I had to get the neighbors to enter my place with me in order to go into my apartment. Finally, I had a good friend come over, and we anointed each door and window with oil, praying for my protection. My anxiety was completely gone, and I never had any fear of entering my apartment after that.

Many months later, I was on a business trip to Kansas City, and I was given a hotel room on the ground floor. Later that night my brain remembered the threatening encounter, and I couldn't sleep. Anxiety filled me. I flipped open my Bible to see if I could find some comfort and my eyes fell on Psalm 121:5: "The Lord is your shade at your right hand" (NIV). I looked up and saw that there was a lamp attached to the wall which was literally above my right hand. I thought, *The Lord is here like this lamp, looking over me and protecting me.* And I was able to fall asleep and slept soundly through the night.

I used to perform music for my church at the time. I usually sung songs I wrote, but I had a strong inclination to sing a song by Kim Hill, "You Alone," which is about how God alone is our comfort. I told the story of feeling afraid, the Bible verse, and the shade over my right hand, and how it all offered a great reminder of God's presence and protection. After church was over, a mom and her little girl came to talk to me. The mom encouraged her daughter, saying, "Go ahead, tell her."

The little girl sheepishly confessed, "Thank you so much for sharing your story and that song. I've been afraid to fall asleep but now I feel better because you were afraid too, and God took care of you. I am encouraged he will take care of me as well."

I didn't like being the victim of a crime, but I'm glad that I was able to receive God's peace and help a little girl do so as well.

"And we know that all things work together for good to them that love God, to them who are the called according to his purpose."
—Romans 8:28, KJV

God Has a Sense of Humor

> What you will receive is directly connected to how you believe.[33]
>
> - Joel Osteen
> *Your Best Life Now*

Becky

Becky is involved with a ministry at her church where once a month they cook, deliver and serve a meal to people living at a shelter for victims of domestic violence. On one such occasion, the team finished cooking the meal, and as was Becky's custom, she shared a short Bible verse with the team and said a little prayer. There happened to be a torrential downpour outside the church as she prayed. She ended the prayer saying, "And God, could you please stop the pouring rain as we load the food and get it there so that the food won't get all wet? Thank you. Amen."

The group gave a little chuckle at the casually stated practical request.

The team delivered the food, served the residents, and did their normal practice of listening and sharing love with the people at the shelter.

---

[33] Joel Osteen, *Your Best Life Now*, (New York, FaithWords, 2004), 22.

When they arrived back at the church, a volunteer approached Becky and asked, "Hey Becky, did you notice what happened?"

"Huh? What?" Becky had no idea what she was talking about.

"Well, actually, I'm a little mad at you. As soon as we stepped out of the church to go deliver the food, it stopped raining just as you prayed. But when we came back it was pouring profusely. Why didn't you ask for God to stop the rain on the way back too?"

Becky had been so busy focusing on the task at hand, she hadn't even noticed that in fact the torrential rains did stop just long enough for them to get the food delivered to the shelter. But yes, they were all drenched from the trip back.

The two laughed and realized that God gave them exactly what Becky asked for, but he gave them a soaking on the way back.

"God does have a sense of humor!" Becky laughed.

"Then our mouth was filled with laughter, and our tongue with shouts of joy; then they said among the nations, "The LORD has done great things for them."
—Psalm 126:2, ESV

Becky has been married to her husband, Patrick, since 1979, and together they have three sons and eight grandchildren. She worked for thirty-five years mostly with special education children and adults, developing programs and materials that were used in schools, day-care centers, and other facilities for children with special needs. She currently is semi-retired, working part time at her church, Praise Assembly in Springfield, Missouri, as a facilities use coordinator. She also volunteers through her church in a number of ministries, including helping their prison ministries, providing assistance to domestic violence victims, veterans and the homeless.

Unseen Miracles

> Our Western mindset has convinced us that we live in a natural, cause-and-effect universe and that the supernatural isn't real, that true miracles not only don't happen, they can't happen.[34]
>
> - Dr. Don Kantel
> *Modern Day Miracles*

Alexandra Georgas

I made friends with an elderly lady who lived alone in my apartment building. She smoked so much her kitchen smelled and the walls were covered with gray soot. She was lonely and thrilled to see me whenever I stopped by to visit.

Eventually I met her son, who expressed much gratitude for my visits with his mother. Some days all three of us would chat over Mama's coffee.

I ran into the son one day at a retail store where he was working. He told me he was recently abruptly laid off after dedicating decades to his company. He was working as temporary holiday help and looking for a new full-time job with benefits.

---

[34] Dr. Don Kantel and Allison C. Restagno, *Modern Day Miracles* (Shippensburg, PA: Destiny Imager, Publishers, 2011), 89.

I told him I would pray for God to give him just what he wanted. I began to pray every day for God to bless him with a job that was even better than the one he had previously.

The next time I saw him was after Christmas at his mother's apartment. He shared that he not only found a new job, but the benefits and pay were much better than his old job. I rejoiced, "How wonderful! That's exactly what I prayed for you! God answered my prayers!"

He doubtfully replied, "Oh I don't know about that. I was just lucky."

There are no miracles for those that have no faith in them.[35]
- French Proverb

I was surprised at his lack of faith. I could see his new job had the mark of God on it, as it was just what I had asked for and was better than the man had even imagined. I had thought he would see from this that there is a God and God cares about him and loves him. But he was blind to seeing God's love for him.

Jesus did a lot of amazing acts that were way more impressive than this one for my neighbor's son. Yet people in

---

[35] Amy Newmark, *Chicken Soup for the Soup: Miracles & Divine Intervention*, (Cos Cob, Connecticut: Chicken Soup for the Soul, 2021), 114.

Jesus's day didn't believe either. I learned a lesson that day that some people just will not accept the miraculous even if it's right in front of their eyes. I feel disappointed for them. They are not enjoying the blessing of receiving God's love for them. But I also know there probably have been thousands of times I missed seeing God's love too. I'm glad God loves us even when we haven't figured that out. I'm thankful for the unseen miracles.

He "is able to do immeasurably more than all we ask or imagine, according to his power that is at work within us."
—Ephesians 3:20, NIV